Other books by DeLinda N. Baker

The Messiah's Imminent Return: Are You Ready?

Throughout both the Old and New Testament there are numerous prophecies pointing to the return of the Messiah in power and glory. The knowledge that the Messiah would someday return and deliver Israel and the saints from the evils of this world has been a tremendous source of encouragement over the ages. The questions have been and continue to be . . . When will Jesus return? Have the signs of his return been fulfilled? Is the Messiah's return imminent? In this study guide, we will explore the scriptures that outline the signs that will precede the return of Jesus Christ in power and glory. In addition to looking at scriptures on the topic, we will look at current and historical events that may be significant. Finally, we will consider how this impacts Christians and our response. Come prepared to dig deep into scriptures and look forward to Jesus' return!

In Search of Truth

There is a surge of 'fake' news overtaking media outlets in the 21st century. Fake news stands in stark contrast to the unbiased objective truth. As integrity and truth become secondary to the desire to sensationalize and sway opinions, we ask ourselves--What is truth? In this devotion, we explore the scriptures to find out what God says about truth. Further, we learn how we can become agents of truth and better discern truth and deception in others.

An ENDURING LEGACY of

Faith

DELINDA N. BAKER

WESTBOW
PRESS®
A DIVISION OF THOMAS NELSON
& ZONDERVAN

WestBow Press books may be ordered through booksellers or by contacting:

WestBow Press
A Division of Thomas Nelson & Zondervan
1663 Liberty Drive
Bloomington, IN 47403
www.westbowpress.com
1 (866) 928-1240

Because of the dynamic nature of the Internet, any web addresses or links contained in this book may have changed since publication and may no longer be valid. The views expressed in this work are solely those of the author and do not necessarily reflect the views of the publisher, and the publisher hereby disclaims any responsibility for them.

Any people depicted in stock imagery provided by Getty Images are models, and such images are being used for illustrative purposes only.
Certain stock imagery © Getty Images.

Unless marked otherwise, all Scripture quotations are taken from The Holy Bible, New International Version®, NIV® Copyright © 1973, 1978, 1984, 2011 by Biblica, Inc.® Used by permission. All rights reserved worldwide.

Scripture quotations marked CEV are taken from the Contemporary English Version®, Copyright © 1995 American Bible Society. All rights reserved.

Scripture quotations marked TLB are taken from The Living Bible, copyright © 1971 by Tyndale House Foundation. Used by permission of Tyndale House Publishers Inc., Carol Stream, Illinois 60188. All rights reserved. The Living Bible, TLB, and the The Living Bible logo are registered trademarks of Tyndale House Publishers.

Scripture quotations marked GW are taken from GOD'S WORD®, © 1995 God's Word to the Nations. Used by permission of God's Word Mission Society.

Edited by Sarah Hobson

ISBN: 978-1-9736-9271-3 (sc)
ISBN: 978-1-9736-9270-6 (e)

Print information available on the last page.

WestBow Press rev. date: 6/9/2020

DEDICATION

To those in my family who for generations have gone before me planting the seed of knowledge of Jesus Christ, faith and obedience to the one true God, and the hope of salvation and eternal life through the power of his resurrection.

To my dear friend, Amy, who encouraged me to write this book, following a series of events in which I spoke on this subject. Thank you for your ongoing support and friendship.

CONTENTS

INTRODUCTION

Have you ever considered what your legacy will be? All of us will face death at some point. When that day comes, we hope that people will fondly remember and miss us. If we are fortunate, we may even leave something tangible behind—perhaps property, a financial inheritance, or a growing family and grandchildren.

Every couple of years my father's brothers, sisters, nieces, nephews, and their extended families gather for a reunion. During this gathering, we usually spend a few minutes remembering those in our family who are no longer with us. Memories are shared, kind words spoken, and even a few tears shed. As I pondered those I love and miss dearly, I started thinking about the legacy I hope to leave behind when I die. How do I want to be remembered? What is the most valuable thing I have to leave my children, grandchildren, and generations that follow?

While I certainly hope that my children know they are loved, leaving a legacy is more than a tangible legacy or an assurance of affection, genetics and common traits. If you are a Christian, there is also a spiritual legacy which includes passing on knowledge of the one true God, planting the seed of faith in the hearts of future generations, showing the way to eternal life, and teaching our children how to live holy righteous lives. It is a legacy of faith and an inheritance of the promises of God, extending beyond the limitations of our mortality and enduring forever.

LEGACIES IN THE BIBLE

Nowadays, you can register with companies which help you trace your family history. You can find out your genealogy, recorded events of your ancestors, and your nationality(-ies) of origin. Some are delighted to find out there was royalty somewhere in their family line. Others find a family history that is less than noteworthy with criminals and family members they would rather not highlight.

The idea of uncovering our legacy is not an idea that began in the twentieth century. When I first started thinking about legacy, I was surprised by how many scriptures reference this subject. These scriptures outline genealogies and with words like generation, children, future and covenant reveal the making of a legacy. There are numerous accounts in the Bible of families and the legacies left from one generation to another. Some of these family trees end in celebration and others in disaster. In the chapters of this book, I will highlight a few of these families. As you read the Bible with this perspective in mind, you will see hundreds of scriptures exhorting us to pass on the knowledge of God to future generations.

Each of us is the product of previous generations. Whether we acknowledge it or not, our legacy began with our past, even before we were born. While we didn't pick the family, skin color, financial status, genetics, or faith of origin we were born into, we can determine our future and our children's future. We can begin today building a legacy that will bear righteous fruit and will bless future generations.

BIRTHING A LEGACY – TELL, TEACH, MODEL

It is important that we teach our children and future generations about God, His attributes, and His commands. How is knowledge passed on from one generation to another? There are many ways that this may occur, but some highlighted in scripture are to tell, teach, and model these lessons to our children. While we can pass on the knowledge of God in any environment, the best one is loving and relational, one rooted in trust, caring, and faithfulness, and one consistently based on truth.

In one of Asaph's proverbs, we read that "we will **tell** the next generation the praiseworthy deeds of the Lord, His power, and the wonders He has done . . . so the next generation would know them, even the children yet to be born, and they in turn would tell their children" (Psalm 78: 4, 6). By telling our children about acts of God, we are relating examples, life experiences, and observations to our children. A lovely Christian woman in our church shared a game she played with her children when they were young. In the evening, after reading scriptures together, they would play "I spy" and talk about where they had seen God during the day. Perhaps they had seen Him in creation: a beautiful sunset, a baby animal, or flowers blooming in the yard. Or perhaps they spied God's handiwork as He protected them from harm, healed a friend, or in a thousand other ways. Not only did she tell her children about God's works, but she showed them how to observe and recount those works for themselves.

Teaching is a little different than telling, in that it is more structured and implies a learning process. In Deuteronomy, parents are encouraged to teach the words of God "to your children, talking about them when you sit at home and when you walk along the road, when you lie down and when you get up" (Deuteronomy 11:19). We teach our children the precepts (laws) and commands of God. This is important to understanding what it means to live righteous lives and to love God through our obedience.

Finally, we pass on information by **modeling** the truth ourselves. There are many axioms in our culture that speak to the importance of living out our beliefs— "your actions say more than your words," we need to "walk the talk," and "our feet show us where our heart is." While it is not always spoken, we know that if we believe something is true then we will display our conviction by acting accordingly. If we know for a fact that a person would be killed if they walk or drive in front of a moving train, we act on that truth by putting guard rails in front of that intersection and warning signs to prevent others from being harmed. We put lifeguards at pools to protect our children from drowning. We hold our children's hand when we cross parking lots or streets. Similarly, our actions of faith, such as reading and studying God's word, praying faithfully, trusting God in difficult times, obeying God's laws and more, confirm our belief in God and model our faith to our children. When Abraham was obedient to God, it was said of him that "his faith and his actions were working together, and his faith was made complete by what he did" (James 2:22). Simply put, "faith by itself, if it is not accompanied by action, is dead" (James 2:17).

We also have an opportunity to impact generations of other families. Just as Jesus expanded salvation beyond the Jews to the Gentiles, we also share the message of salvation beyond our immediate families to others. A scripture referred to as the Great Commission was given to the apostles before Jesus ascended into Heaven. Matthew 28:19-20 commanded the apostles to "go and make disciples of **all** nations, baptizing them in the name of the Father and of the Son and of the Holy Spirit, and teaching them to obey everything I have commanded you." As we tell, teach, and model the gospel of salvation and our faith to our friends, neighbors, co-workers, and even strangers, we fulfill the Great Commission.

HOW DOES IT WORK

In the chapters that follow, we will consider what it means to build a legacy that will span future generations. We will see that God's commitment to us is timeless. He has been and will be present from the beginning to the end of time. He has fellowshipped with the men and women He has called to serve Him and has spoken to them about future generations. We can be sure that the promises and covenants God has made with His people will endure and be fulfilled, whether we live to see it or not.

Next, we will look at how previous generations and outside influences affect our actions and outlook. In some cases, we may need to unravel negative influences and change the pattern for future generations. In other cases, we will build on the foundation left by our forefathers.

Having established God's role in our lives and the influence others have had on us, we will shift our focus to our responsibility going forward. When we are faithful to live out our commitment to God, we build families that know and love God. Future generations are blessed by this righteous heritage. Also, we will teach generations how to live righteously by passing on morals and values.

And finally, we will reflect on the far-reaching impact of our legacy. The Bible teaches that not only will our legacy bless future generations, but that the righteous are investing in a future that spans eternity. It is exciting that you and I can have an impact with such breadth and scope of future generations by faithfully living according to God's will.

At the end of each chapter there will be a brief prayer and some questions as you internalize and reflect on the application of the topics discussed.

A GENERATIONAL IMPRINT

A legacy's imprint resides in all of our lives. While it doesn't absolutely define us, we can't deny its effect on how we think, our priorities, and foundation. Whether it be one of righteousness or evil, the legacy we leave behind will have an imprint on those who follow us.

The purpose of this book is to encourage and re-focus our thinking about leaving an intentional legacy, one that will endure and be built on a firm foundation—a legacy that will bring glory to God.

Reflections and Personal Study

Reflect on the main topics covered in the chapter.
Read and meditate on supporting scriptures.
Consider how this applies to your personal life.

Topic: For each of us there is a physical and a spiritual legacy.

Application: How do you want to be remembered when you die?

Application: List 2-3 examples of a tangible and/or physical legacy.

Application: List 2-3 examples of a spiritual legacy.

Legacies in the Bible
Topic: Legacy is talked about in the Bible, through scriptures, individual lives, and family lines.

Birthing a Legacy
Topic: Knowledge about God is passed on from one generation to another through telling, teaching, and modeling.

Scripture: Read Psalm 78:4-6. The Hebrew word for "tell" is *caphar*, meaning to declare, show forth, or tell. What should we tell our children?

Scripture: Read Deuteronomy 11:19. The Hebrew word for "teach" is *lamad*, meaning to instruct, learn, or provide skillful teaching with the intent to stimulate an action or reaction. What should we teach our children?

What is the difference between telling and teaching?

Scripture: Read James 2:17-20. What actions should we model for our children?

In the infinite wisdom of the Lord of all the earth, each event falls with exact precision into its proper place in the unfolding of His divine plan. Nothing, however small, however strange, occurs without His ordering or without its particular fitness for its place in the working out of His purpose; and the end of all shall be the manifestation of His glory, and the accumulation of His praise.

~ B.B. Warfield
Professor of Theology, 4th Principal of
Princeton Theological Seminary,
1851-1921

1

A GOD FOR GENERATIONS

This is My name forever, the name you shall
call Me from generation to generation.
—*Exodus 3:15*

IT IS COMMON KNOWLEDGE IN BUILDING A HOUSE THAT foundation is essential to a stable structure. As we learn in Matthew 7:24-27, a house built on a firm foundation (the Word of God) will not fall during the storms of life, but a house built on a shaky foundation (those who disregard God's Word) will not be able to withstand the storms. If we care about the strength, endurability, and wisdom of future generations, it is important that those who believe and walk with God leave a legacy of a firm foundation.

As we read the Old Testament, we learn that God had a relationship with the forefathers of our faith. He spoke with them, ate with them, and walked with them. He is the God of our fathers.

To the faithful individuals who were chosen by God, He made covenants with them. He made promises and commitments to our forefathers that would have a lasting impact on the chosen people of God. He is a God of covenants.

The one true God, who is the Alpha and Omega, is a God who was with His people in the past, who is with them in the present, and One who will be there for future generations. God has a perspective that looks across all generations. His purpose and plan not only impacts our lifespans, but those of our children and children's children, even to eternity. He is a God of purpose.

GOD OF OUR FATHERS

Since the first day people were created and placed on this earth, God has made Himself known. It began with a walk in the garden of Eden with Adam and Eve. From the beginning of creation, God's plan was to have a warm loving relationship with mankind. Even though this plan was interrupted by the introduction of disobedience (sin) into the world, this is still God's plan. Through His son, Jesus, restoration of this relationship is possible.

The Bible teaches that God has always existed and always will exist. When asked His name in Exodus 3:14, God answered simply "I am." This fundamental belief that God exists and created life, this world, this universe, and all things unseen must be passed on to our children. Just as a foundation is essential in building a house, knowing that God exists is key to understanding His majesty, worshiping Him, and having fellowship with Him.

There are some in our culture who actively resist this simple foundational belief. They often teach that the uniqueness of individuals, the earth and its elements, and the expanse of the skies are an accidental occurrence from a mathematically slight chance of the right combination of events, evolution, and dominance. Without God, people are left to depend on themselves in fighting the battles of life. Our value is limited to our short lifespan of this earth, so we may as well focus our energies on living for today. Why worry about a future that is defined by chance?

Nothing can be further from the truth. God does exist. He has a purpose for our lives. He is actively overseeing creation, its development, and our lives. Just as in the days of Adam and Eve, God still desires a relationship with each of us. The scriptures teach us that we are more than a vapor, that our lives do matter and our actions have consequences both in our lifetimes and eternally. With this perspective, suddenly legacy becomes very important. What we teach our children and leave behind has value.

As Jacob lay on his deathbed, he blessed Joseph's sons. "May the God before whom my fathers Abraham and Isaac walked faithfully, the God who has been my shepherd all my life to this day, the Angel who has delivered me from all harm—may He bless these boys. May they be called by my name and the names of my fathers Abraham and Isaac, and may they increase greatly on the earth" (Genesis 48:15-16). This blessing summed up a legacy of a lasting and enduring relationship with God the Father that had been and was still being passed from one generation to the next.

GOD OF COVENANTS

In an age of live-for-the-moment gratification, the idea of making of covenant, a binding agreement for an extended period, runs contrary to our thinking. Yet God's longstanding relationship with His people is underscored with promises and commitment. In the Old Testament, we see many of these covenants made with men and women of faith. Since God is faithful and trustworthy, His covenants are a promise of an eventual and certain outcome. Despite the temporary wanderings and unfaithfulness that would be displayed by future generations, covenants lead God's people to a predestined path of fulfillment that involves repentance, forgiveness, restoration, and renewal.

> Know therefore that the Lord your God is God; He is the faithful God, keeping His covenant of love to a thousand generations of those who love Him and keep His commandments. (Deuteronomy 7:9)

God revealed to Adam mankind's original purpose to subdue the Earth and its creatures, warning him that the consequence of rebellion would be hardship, pain, and death (Genesis 3:16-19). After the world-wide flood, God promised Noah, a descendant of Adam, that He would never destroy mankind again by a flood (Genesis 8:21). Many years later, God promised Abraham, a descendant of Noah, that he would become the father of nations and that the world would be blessed by his seed (Genesis 15:4–21). To Moses, from the tribe of Levi (one of the grandsons of Abraham), He gave the Ten Commandments, along with the conditional promise of blessing to those who obeyed (Deuteronomy 11:26–28). To David, also from the lineage of Abraham, He promised an eternal kingdom (2 Samuel 7:12-13). To the prophet Jeremiah, He promised restoration and forgiveness to future generations through the Messiah, a descendant of David (Jeremiah 31:31–34). These covenants were not idle agreements. Instead, they were promised by a God who makes binding covenants with His people and promises to restore, protect and love them, to bring salvation, and to never forget them.

As Christians, we inherit God's covenants along with the forefathers of our faith. "And you are heirs of the prophets and of the covenant God made with your fathers" (Acts 3:25). As individuals saved by grace, we must live in obedience and faith, thus proving we are heirs of God's promise.

GOD OF PURPOSE

Every year we celebrate the ending of one year and the beginning of another on New Year's Eve. We anxiously watch the clock and count down the minutes to the next year. Many of us make resolutions for the new year with promises of renewed purpose and determination. But as the months go by, few of us actually see those resolutions fulfilled.

This stands in stark contrast to the resolutions of God. God has set His purpose in the hearts of individuals and carries it out. "Who has done this and carried it through, calling forth the generations from the beginning? I, the Lord—with the first of them and with the last—I am He" (Isaiah 41:4).

Consider the full weight of this proclamation from Isaiah.

God was "with the first of them and with the last." He has called forth "generations from the beginning" and "carried it through." As members of the body of Christ, we are part of the far-reaching purpose of God which spans generations.

What is this purpose? God has a plan for restoration and eternal fellowship with him. In Romans 8, His plan for our good is summarized as being "conformed to the image of His Son, that He might be the firstborn among many brothers and sisters" (verse 29). This transformation is made possible through justification, the redemption of our bodies, and glorification by the blood of Christ.

There are other things that God desires for His children as well. In scripture we find that God desires that His Word lives in our hearts (Deuteronomy 11:18) and that He desires harmony with mankind, the earth, and its creatures (Romans 8:19). God's purpose for each of us is that we experience joy, peace (Romans 15:13) in our personal lives, but that we also live beyond ourselves and exude His attributes of compassion, mercy, and love to others.

> But the plans of the Lord stand firm forever, the purposes
> of His heart through all generations. (Psalm 33:11)

Some of God's purposes will be fulfilled in our lifetimes as we walk holy and uprightly with Him. As for the remainder of His plan, we can be assured that it will be fulfilled when Satan and the evils in our world are conquered by His Son, Jesus, as He returns to this earth in power and glory.

We have inherited an incredible blessing from God through His Son. However, as we look closer at Psalm 33, we see that it is not God's plan that we keep this blessing to ourselves. In the phrase, "through all generations," we unveil how God's purpose is furthered as we pass on the underlying faith and teachings that make it possible for future generations to share in this blessing. We cannot accept Christ for our children, nor can we save our children from eternal judgment. However, we can share with our family the gospel of Christ and the reason for our faith, prayerfully hoping that their hearts will be softened and that they too will know God, so that they too will inherit His blessings.

As King David's reign was coming to an end, he gathered the provisions needed to build a temple for God. His heart was touched by the generous giving of his people to make this incredible house of worship a reality—gold, precious metals, rare gems, artifacts, and tapestries, along with a donation of their time and skills. He thanked God, "Lord our God, all this abundance that we have provided for building You a temple for Your Holy Name comes from Your hand, and all of it belongs to You ... and now I have seen with joy how willingly Your people who are here have given to You" (1 Chronicles 29:16-17). It gave him immeasurable joy to see his people express their love for God. Yet David was not a man who thought only of today, he looked to the future as his heartfelt prayer continued, "Lord, the God of our fathers Abraham, Isaac and Israel, keep these desires and thoughts in the hearts of Your people forever, and keep their hearts loyal to You" (verse 18). He also prayed for his son Solomon, desiring only the very best for his son, he wisely asked God to give his son the one thing he treasured most, the one thing his son could count on, the one thing that would never run out—a deep and abiding relationship with God as he began the arduous task of building the temple. "And give my son Solomon the wholehearted devotion to keep Your commands, statutes and decrees" (verse 19).

This heartfelt prayer shows us how we can pray for future generations. We can pray that God's people and our descendants will have generous hearts openly giving of their possessions, talent and wealth to God. We can pray that God's desires and thoughts will be in their hearts forever. Finally, we can pray that they will be wholeheartedly devoted to keeping God's commands.

ABRAHAM'S LEGACY: FAITH, A SON, AND A NATION

Much is said in the scripture about Abraham, the father of Israel. However, one key word sums up his legacy—faith. Abraham's faith was characterized by trust and obedience. This is the kind of faith God is looking for from His people. Because of his exemplary faith, God promised to make Abraham's children into a great and powerful nation and that a descendant from his family line would bless all the people of the earth. God directed Abraham to continue keeping His covenants, both he and his descendants for generations to come.

Abraham's journey of faith was not an easy one. In Abraham's day, a man's perpetuity was assured when a male heir was born into the family. Abraham assumed God's promise to make his children into a great and powerful nation meant that he and his wife, Sarah, would actually have children. Abraham waited and hoped for what seemed an eternity for a child, but as he and his wife Sarah grew older, their hopes for a family began to diminish. Despite the loss of all hope in an heir as their bodies continued to age, Abraham believed God. He did not know how God would keep His promise, but he knew God was faithful and this unwavering faith was counted as "righteousness" (Romans 4:30).

On a day just like any other, he and Sarah had a few unexpected guests drop by (Genesis 18:1-15). As was the custom, they offered these travelers food, water, and a place to rest. As they sat together chatting under a shade tree, it became evident that one of these men was not an ordinary visitor. The visitor gave them a message from God, they were going to have a son. At first, Sarah laughed and as she wondered how she and her husband, now well beyond child bearing years, would have a child. But the visitor was insistent and true to his word, a child was born to Sarah and Abraham within the year.

They were joyful beyond words and rejoiced with their friends. They felt young again and happily raised their son, Isaac. The years passed and soon Isaac was twelve-years-old. Abraham felt sure this child was the fulfillment of God's promise to him. Then another day came, this time a day of testing. As Abraham worshiped God, God commanded him to take Isaac to the altar and sacrifice him (Genesis 22:1-2). Abraham may have teared up as he considered the implications of this command, placing his precious son on an altar.

As he gained control of his emotions, he remembered how big his God was and that nothing is impossible with God.

Finally, with some difficulty, a decision was made to trust and obey God. Abraham chose to be obedient to God, even to the point of sacrificing his son. He believed God's promise that future generations would come from his lineage. Even if he did not know how God would fulfill this, he was determined to be faithful. This deep imbedded trust in God empowered him to put one foot in front of the other as he marched toward the altar with his beloved son.

Isaac was old enough that he was able to help his father carry the wood and rope on his back (Genesis 22:6). As they approached the altar, Isaac innocently asked "where is the lamb for the burnt offering?" Abraham answered, "God will provide." Once they arrived, he bound Isaac with ropes and placed him on the altar. Imagine what was going through Isaac's mind! Then God spoke: "Now I know that you fear God, because you have not withheld from Me your son, your only son" (verse 12). Then a ram appeared in the thicket. Abraham quickly removed his son and replaced him with the ram, who was then sacrificed.

Isaac must have learned some important lessons that day. He knew how deeply his mother and father loved him. His father had told him about God's promise and told him that he was a very special child. He had gone to the altar many times with his father and witnessed his father's obedience to God and what it meant to walk by faith. He witnessed God's provision of a sacrificial ram to take his place. These were lessons that would be passed down to generations. Just as God promised to Abraham, Isaac would one day become the father of Jacob, who would become the father of a nation, Israel, which would become a great and powerful nation that would bless all the nations of the earth (Genesis 18:18).

Through Abraham's family lineage, a Messiah would be born to save people and reconcile them to God. "Therefore, the promise comes by faith, so that it may be by grace and may be guaranteed to all Abraham's offspring—not only to those who are of the law but also to those who have the faith of Abraham. He is the father of us all" (Romans 4:16). "In other words, it is not the children by physical descent who are God's children, but it is the children of the promise who are regarded as Abraham's offspring" (Romans 9:8). Because of his faith, Abraham passed on an incredible legacy to his son, his grandchildren, and generations to follow.

A SOLID FOUNDATION

Without a good foundation, faith will not endure the storms of life. Families need strength in conviction, prayer, resolve, understanding, body, and spirit. Where does all this strength come from? Ourselves? Absolutely not! We can be certain that when we are left to our own resources, it will not take long before we encounter the limitations of our abilities and will.

"It is God who arms me with strength and keeps my way secure" (Psalm 18:32). In establishing a foundation for a legacy, we must pass on an accurate and true image of God. Just as God is the source of our strength, His attributes console and comfort us. The God of our fathers is a loving and kind God. He is merciful and long suffering, patiently enduring our sins while waiting for repentance. He is forgiving and compassionate. "For the Lord is good and His love endures forever; His faithfulness continues through all generations" (Psalm 100:5). Knowing that God is all of these things encourages us to seek fellowship with Him, to share our burdens with Him, and to trust Him to lovingly hear and answer our prayers.

He is a God of generations. God is not just living in and for the present. He is the eternal Alpha and Omega, connecting the past, present, and future.

Likewise, we should not live one-dimensional lives, absorbed by self and focused only on the present. We also should have a perspective of past, present and future. We should make efforts to understand how past generations have impacted us. Our present lives should be characterized by righteousness, obedience to God and a growing faith. Finally, we should be thoughtful and intentional, understanding how our actions will impact future generations.

Prayer: Heavenly Father, You are Alpha and Omega and see the full span of time from its beginning to the end. Because You are faithful and trustworthy, we know that Your plans for hope and a future (Jeremiah 29:11) are certain to be fulfilled. Give us courage, Lord, to face each day knowing that You are able to complete the work of salvation and transformation in each of us. Help us Lord to be faithful to grow in love and obedience to You. Please show us how to leave a legacy of faith and righteousness to future generations. Amen.

Reflections and Personal Study

Reflect on the main topics covered in the chapter.
Read and meditate on supporting scriptures.
Consider how this applies to your personal life.

God of our Fathers
Topic: God had a relationship with the forefathers of our faith.

Scripture: Read Genesis 48:15-16. Why is it important that one generation teach the one that follows about God's existence?

Application: How does passing on and/or receiving a spiritual legacy impact one's relationship with God?

God of Covenants
Topic: God made covenants with the forefathers of our faith that impacted future generations.

Scripture: Read Deuteronomy 7:9. Why are covenants important to our relationship with God?

Scripture: Read Acts 3:25. As Christians, do we inherit God's covenants that were made with the forefathers of our faith?

God of Purpose

Topic: God has a perspective that looks across all generations – past, present and future.

Topic: God has a plan for restoration and eternal fellowship with him.

Scripture: Read Psalm 33:11. What are the purposes and plans of God that will stand forever?

Abraham's Legacy

Topic: Abraham's faith was characterized by trust and obedience.

Scripture: Read Genesis 22:1-18. What lessons do you learn from Abraham's response to God's command?

Application: What do you think Isaac took away from this experience?

Application: What was the far-reaching impact of Abraham's decision to obey God?

A Solid Foundation

Topic: In establishing a foundation for a legacy, we must pass on an accurate and true image of God.

Application: List 2 or 3 beliefs about God passed down to you from previous generations that have had a strong influence on your understanding of God.

Application: List 2 or 3 of God's promises that have a direct impact your family?

Application: List 2 or 3 of God's purpose and plans that you believe are meant for you and your descendants?

Each day of our lives we make deposits in the memory banks of our children.

~ Chuck Swindoll
Christian Author and Pastor,
Founder *Insight for Living*, 1934-today

2

A LEGACY INHERITED

*From everlasting to everlasting the Lord's love is
with those who fear Him, and His righteousness with
their children's children—with those who keep His
covenant and remember to obey His precepts.*
— *Psalm 103:17-18*

I OFTEN THINK OF THE LEGACY LEFT TO ME. MY PARENTS
and grandparents were Christians. My great-grandparents and
great-great grandparents were Christians. At least four generations
that I know of were Christians and there were probably more. I
was brought up in a home where love was evident. Whether sitting
around a table for a meal, showing support for sports activities or
school events, or simply spending time together, I always felt the love
and acceptance of my parents. On those occasions where discipline
was needed, my parents metered the appropriate punishment with
a restraint tempered by love, a calm explanation of right and wrong
behavior, and soon after forgiveness. I was one of the lucky ones in
life.

Many others in this world have not had the blessing of loving
parents. For them, memories may not be as warm. Forgiveness
may be difficult. Bad parenting patterns may be difficult to unlearn
and change. Yet, regardless of our upbringing, once we make the

decision to follow God's path for our lives, we share the opportunity to become people who bequeath a blessing to our children and future generations. That is one of the remarkable gifts of salvation through Christ, that we are made new. This newness regenerates our family legacy, fresh and full of hope.

Families can leave a legacy that is positive or negative. For the righteous, the legacy is one of knowing God, being blessed by God, and inheriting the promises of God. For the unrighteous, the legacy is one of not being taught about God, bad habits and sinful behavior, which will ultimately incur the wrath of God.

When you consider the impact your family history has had on you—how you feel about yourself and others, habits and behaviors, your faith or lack of faith in an all-powerful God, and so much more—it is not difficult to see why legacy is important to future generations. Having a secure legacy gives us a sense of belonging, security, strength, purpose, and love. It gives us the courage to pursue paths of opportunity and selflessness and teaches us values and morals.

Our legacy starts with what we have received from generations past, but it ends with what we leave to future generations.

ADAM'S LEGACY: DISOBEDIENCE, SIN, AND DEATH

The life of Adam and his fall from grace is one of the sad notes in history. Imagine that your legacy is one which has doomed mankind to suffering and judgment. As a result of Adam and Eve's sin, the ground was cursed, pain and toil would define mankind's work and all people would ultimately face death (Genesis 3:17-19). Even though God warned them of the consequence of disobedience, it is likely that Adam and Eve did not expect their actions would have such a far-reaching impact.

From the day Adam and Eve opened their eyes, they had a very special bond with God. There was an honesty there. Nothing was hidden. Adam and Eve could be totally transparent in their thoughts and actions. They were naked before God and unashamed (Genesis 2:25).

Plants all around them were perfectly formed and thriving. "Streams came up from the earth and watered the whole surface of the ground" (Genesis 2:6). They had plenty of food, lived in paradise, and were free to make choices. Daily, God walked in the garden and conversed with Adam (Genesis 3:8). While we don't know what they talked about, you can imagine Adam telling God about his day, sharing his dreams and interests, asking advice, and admiring the intricacies of God's creation.

God gave Adam the privilege of naming the animals that filled the earth (Genesis 2:20). The purpose of mankind was established: to rule "over the fish in the sea and the birds in the sky, over the livestock and all the wild animals, and over all the creatures that move along the ground" (Genesis 1:26). This perfect planet was not only his home, but it was his responsibility to care for it. It was akin to a father handing down part of the family business for the children to manage and God called this "good."

In addition to giving Adam responsibilities and direction, God also established boundaries. "Don't eat of this one tree in the garden," He said (Genesis 2:17). Just as a parent and child lovingly relate to one another, Adam had a relationship with his creator and father, God. But a dark day was looming on the horizon, a day when Adam would rebel against God.

Both Adam and Eve chose to disobey God. Eve was the first to listen to the enticement from the serpent, "You will not certainly die . . . eat from it . . . and you will be like God, knowing good and evil" (Genesis 3:4-5). Adam then joined Eve and also willingly ate from the tree. They no sooner took a bite, then their eyes were opened. Despite Satan's alluring promise, the Bible never said that they knew as much as God. It was also untrue that they would not die. Everything the serpent had said was a lie! Their eyes were opened alright, but to their own indiscretions. Now they realized they were naked and they were ashamed. Now they felt they had to hide from God and their relationship with Him was strained. Soon they would face the consequence of their actions and be banned from the paradise they had enjoyed.

You and I may think we would have acted differently. Perhaps we think that we would be satisfied with all that God had provided, would not be tempted, and would simply obey God. I doubt it. We are Adam's children and unfortunately bear a family resemblance when it comes to our propensity to sin.

The Bible teaches us the consequences of living a sinful life. God will hide His face from the perverse (Deuteronomy 32:20). If you persist in sin, you, your children, your work, and many aspects of your life will be cursed (Deuteronomy 28:15). You will be defeated by your enemies and live in bondage to your sins (Deuteronomy 28:25; Romans 7:23). A sinful life is one that pushes God away and is restricted by the boundaries of our flesh and ability. It is a life without hope and a future (Psalm 37:38). Sinners will be destroyed and receive punishment on the day of judgment (2 Peter 2:9).

Perhaps our sins will not have the far-reaching impact of Adam and Eve's sin, but the fact that their disobedience changed the course for mankind is a sobering reminder of the importance of our decisions. We need to remember this the next time we are tempted to disobey God. While God's plan for His children was paradise and an inheritance, Satan's empty promises lead to separation and shame.

INHERITANCE FOR RIGHTEOUS

There is a huge blessing in store for the righteous, those who love God and keep His commandments. God will show His love to a thousand generations that follow, forgiving wickedness, rebellion, and sin. God pronounced this blessing twice to Moses, once in Exodus 20 as He handed down the Ten Commandments; and again, in Exodus 34, when Moses returned to Mt. Sinai, to receive the Commandments a second time (after the Israelites sinned). At such a critical time, when God was giving a short list of rules for His people to follow, He expressed the enormous love He has for His people, far outweighing the penalty of those who rejected Him! Think about it. He said He would punish the children of the guilty to the third and fourth generation, but He would maintain love to a thousand generations of those who love Him and keep His commandments (Exodus 20:4-6; Exodus 34:6-7). The blessing extended much further (1,000 generations) in comparison to the punishment (three to four generations). The breadth of this impact punctuated the importance of keeping God's commandments.

When I read the history of the generation who received the commandments of God through Moses, it becomes evident that sharing the knowledge of God to our families is a sacred privilege and responsibility. In teaching our children what it means to know God and keep His commands, we are passing down the essential components to relating to God and living a holy and blessed life. The Creator who gave us life, Who knows our every cell, DNA, chromosome, and component of our being, Who understands exactly how we tick and what will give us the most fulfillment, is the One who says we and future generations will be blessed by loving and obeying Him.

Knowing God's promise, we should take stock of what we are teaching our children. In Psalm 71:18, we are told to declare God's power and mighty acts to future generations. Consider some of the promises that come through loving and obeying God . . .

- Whoever loves God is known by God (1 Corinthians 8:3)
- Those who seek God will receive blessing and vindication (Psalm 24:5-6)
- If you keep God's decrees and commands, it will go well with you and your children (Deuteronomy 4:40, 5:29)
- God's mercy extends to those who fear Him (Luke 1:50)

Look carefully one more time at these promises and you will see that they are not only for the individual who loves God but also for future generations. Psalm 24:5 says the blessing is for the generation who seeks God. Deuteronomy 4:40 says it will go well for you and your children. Luke 1:50 says God's mercy extends from generation to generation. If we are faithful to teach our children the ways of God, there are many blessings that await future generations. What a tremendous legacy to leave our children and grandchildren, to be blessed by God.

NOAH'S LEGACY: RESCUE, A SIGN, AND A FRESH START

Have you ever felt like everywhere you looked, you were surrounded by people who don't know or understand God? There was a time on earth when this was literally true. It's hard to believe that mankind could move from intimate fellowship and walking in the garden with God, to disobedience, to falling further down the steep and slippery slope of sin until it pervaded every aspect of life. Yes, those who followed God were a minority during these times. There was only a flicker of hope in a man named Noah.

Noah was born several generations after Adam. Adam and Eve had many children after Cain and Abel. When Adam was 130 years old, he had a son named Seth. Seth's name means "appointed one." While Adam's other son Cain, who murdered Abel, became the father of deceitful and murderous generations, Seth in contrast became the father of many righteous individuals. Many generations followed as outlined in Genesis 5: Adam was the father of Seth, who was the father of Enosh, who was the father of Kenan, who was the father of Mahalalel, who was the father of Jared, who was the father of Enoch, who was the father of Methuselah, who was the father of Lamech, who was the father of Noah. In this lengthy family line, Noah's great-grandfather Enoch was said to have "walked faithfully with God" and while all others in his family line "died," Enoch was simply "taken away by God" (verse 24) almost 70 years before Noah's birth. Though Noah never met Enoch, his father Lamech lived during Enoch's last 90 years. While the Bible doesn't speak of their relationship, possibly during this time Lamech and his grandfather had conversations in which Enoch testified to his great love for God.

When Noah was born, his father Lamech said that this young son would "comfort us in the labor and painful toil of our hands" (Genesis 5:29). Like his great-grandfather Enoch, Noah was a righteous man who walked "faithfully with God" and "did everything just as God commanded him" (Genesis 6: 9, 22). Because of his faithful obedience, he would indeed become a source of great comfort and hope.

The day came when this faith was tested. The earth had become corrupt and full of violence to the point "God regretted that He had made humans" (Genesis 6:6). God went to Noah and told him of His plan to wipe out mankind with a flood. He instructed Noah to build an ark and gave him detailed instructions for the task. God also instructed Noah to prepare for two of each animal to board the ark, along with his family. Only Noah's family and these animals would be spared God's judgment on the earth and mankind. A disaster of such proportion today would be referred to as a global catastrophe.

Noah's response to such news wasn't to bask in his good fortune to be selected to survive. It wasn't to run out and warn as many neighbors as possible. It wasn't to shake his head in disbelief, leaning on his own understanding and past experience instead of God's word. In Genesis 6:22, the Bible simply tells us that "Noah did everything just as God commanded him." Noah's commitment to God was proven by his actions and unwavering obedience. As it says in Hebrews 11, "by his faith he condemned the world and became heir of the righteousness that is in keeping with faith" (verse 7).

Just as God had said, the rains and flood soon came. Only Noah, his sons, their wives, and animals selected by God survived. All other life on earth was wiped clean (Genesis 7:23). As Noah emerged from the ark onto dry land, almost a year after the devastating event, his first action was worship (Genesis 8:20). On that day, God formed a covenant with Noah, promising that He would never again destroy the earth by a flood and set a rainbow in the sky to remind Noah of this promise. While sin would unfortunately once again penetrate the world, Noah's faith and obedience became an example for many.

DeLinda N. Baker

PLANTING THE SEED

The Bible speaks of the impact of a righteous individual on thousands of generations. That is really big! I know that I feel very inconsequential and to think that my actions might impact my family for years to come is a big responsibility, one that if I'm honest, I hesitate to claim. I know my own limitations and propensity to make mistakes. Only by God's grace is such an impact even possible.

How can the next generation receive God's blessing if they don't know Him? We must be intentional in sharing the good news to our children and modeling what it looks like to follow God. While we are imperfect and certainly will make mistakes along the way, we can show the path to forgiveness and redemption through Jesus. We can teach our children to seek, love, and obey God first and foremost. We can pray for our families and future generations, entrusting their future to God. Planting these habits and priority in their minds, actions and hearts will cultivate the seed that will grow a harvest for generations.

You can change the course for future generations. Make a decision today to not leave an unhappy and sinful inheritance to your children. Instead, repent and return to God's ways, thus leaving an inheritance of righteousness.

Prayer: Lord, I thank You for my family – for my parents, for my children, and grandchildren, and for my many relatives. You have blessed me with each of them and with an opportunity to have a lasting impact on future generations. Empower me by Your grace and Holy Spirit to be faithful to share the good news of Jesus, to be a beacon of light to my family and to direct them to the truth in Your Word. In Jesus name I pray, Amen.

Reflections and Personal Study

Reflect on the main topics covered in the chapter.
Read and meditate on supporting scriptures.
Consider how this applies to your personal life.

Topic: Families can leave a legacy that is positive or negative.

Application: List a few of the traditions and beliefs, both cultural and spiritual, that have been passed down through your family. Do you consider these influences to have been positive or negative?

Application: Think about your spiritual legacy. Start a list of those who have influenced you in your faith.

Adam's Legacy
Topic: As a result of Adam and Eve's sin, the ground was cursed, pain and toil would define mankind's work and all people would ultimately face death.

Scripture: Read Genesis 3:1-10. What was the root sin of Adam and Eve? Why did they eat the apple? How did their sin impact future generations?

Inheritance for the Righteous

Topic: God will show His love to a thousand generations that follow, forgiving wickedness, rebellion, and sin.

Scripture: Read Exodus 34:6-7. What is the blessing that will be inherited by future generations?

Application: List some of the other promises that the righteous will inherit.

Noah's Legacy

Topic: Noah's commitment to God was proven by his actions and unwavering obedience.

Scripture: Read Genesis 6:22. What was Noah's response to the devastating news that God would destroy the world?

Scripture: How did God view Noah's obedience (Hebrews 11:7)?

Planting the Seed

Topic: We must be intentional in sharing the good news to our children and modeling what it looks like to follow God.

Application: How can each of us plant the seed of righteousness in our families and those who God brings into our lives?

There is no knowing that does not begin with knowing God.

~ John Calvin
French Theologian, Pastor, 1509-1564

3

A LEGACY OF KNOWING GOD

*"You are My witnesses," declares the Lord, "and My
servant whom I have chosen, so that you may know and
believe Me and understand that I am He. Before Me no
god was formed, nor will there be one after Me. I, even
I, am the Lord, and apart from Me there is no savior.*
— Isaiah 43:10-11

O UR INITIAL UNDERSTANDING OF GOD, HIS
character and His works, is often based on our parent's
perception of God. If they believed in a God who was
powerful, all-knowing, gracious, loving, and more, in other words
their God was greater than the circumstances and world around
them, this was shown to us by their faith and confidence in God
as they responded to difficult situations and daily challenges. If
their god was small, subservient to mankind's whim and definition,
then this was also evident by their lack of faith and dependence on
themselves and good fortune.

If you want your children and future generations to know God,
then you must be intentional about sharing your faith and beliefs with
your family. We are God's chosen witnesses with a primary mission:
that our family and others may know, believe, and understand God
and His saving power (Isaiah 43:10-11). We have both the privilege

and responsibility to be the first, and possibly most influential, voices in our children's lives.

BELIEF IN GOD

Fundamental to believing in God is the core faith that God exists. Creation, the works of God, and a spiritual awareness in our inner beings are among the many scriptural and logical arguments that have been given to support the existence of God.

Psalm 19 teaches us that creation testifies to the glory of God: "The heavens declare the glory of God; the skies proclaim the work of His hands. Day after day they pour forth speech; night after night they reveal knowledge" (verses 1-2). God created the earth, all of its elements, the creatures that walk on its face and swim in its oceans. God created the heavens and the expanse of the universe, the galaxies, stars, planets and celestial bodies that orbit them, comets and meteors, black holes, and other phenomena yet to be discovered. God created all living beings both in heaven and on earth, those seen and unseen, and the vegetation and waters on our planet. All of this came into being through His word, He spoke and it happened. As we observe the world around us and the universe beyond, we are humbled by the power of a mighty Creator.

This and other aspects of creation confirm God's eternal power and divine nature (Romans 1:20). As scientists search other galaxies for another planet that is similar to Earth in its ability to support life, we are learning that Earth is much rarer than initially thought. Everything from the perfect positioning of the Earth's orbit, to the atmosphere and land conditions needed to support life, to the existence of life organisms have overcome astronomical odds for the likelihood of their occurrence. The unique nature of Earth, along with the order and classifications that are evident in plant and animal species on Earth, support the existence of an intelligent and intentional Creator.

We also know God exists by His works: "Many, Lord my God,

are the wonders You have done" (Psalm 40:5). These mighty works not only include creation, but also the countless works and miracles recorded in the scriptures. Consider God's powerful works in nature, such as stopping the sun in the sky for a day, a global flood wiping out mankind, hail and brimstone falling from the sky destroying a city, or even the Lord walking on water. God worked on behalf of the Israelites, defeating armies against unsurmountable odds, protecting their sovereignty as a nation, and fulfilling prophecies. Miracles affecting individuals are also recorded, such as the provision of basic necessities during times of need, physical healing from disease and crippling birth defects, expulsion of demons, and even resurrection from the dead. These are only a few examples of the many powerful acts of God recorded in the Bible. The works of God have been evident throughout history and are still happening today. Many testimonies have been shared of answered prayers: jobs provided, unexplainable healing, help and finances miraculously appearing, delivery from prison, and many more. "All Your works praise You, Lord; Your faithful people extol You" (Psalm 145:10).

Finally, God has placed a spiritual awareness in each of us that is evident in our religious beliefs, understanding of good and evil, and perceived life beyond death. There is a human inclination to want to worship a god, as evidenced by the broad belief in god(s) across nations and cultures that has existed throughout history. While not everyone believes in the God of Israel, religions around the world worship a supreme being or several gods, and in some cases a man-made god or idol. There also appears to be a universal sense of right and wrong. In most cultures, murder, lying, stealing, and immorality are rejected as evil or harmful. On the other end of the spectrum, kindness, mercy, love, and good deeds are universally commended as praiseworthy and admirable. Finally, there is a mysterious feeling in each of us that there is more to come beyond our life and time on Earth. Ecclesiastes 3 tells us that God has "set eternity in the human heart" (verse 11). These intangible feelings and inclinations toward divinity, morality and eternity support an innate awareness placed in our souls by the Creator.

For some, if they cannot see, touch, and feel God, they assume He doesn't exist except in our minds. Yet every day we see the evidence of God's existence in the world around us. An analogy that might be familiar is air. Does anyone doubt there is breathable air all around us? Yet we can't see, touch or feel it. However, we can see the effects of our atmosphere in wind and weather. Likewise, while we can't see God, we can see and feel the effect of His existence in creation, our lives, and even to the depth of our souls.

God's vitality is evident every day. We must take the time to observe God in the world around us. This is essential to nurturing our belief in a God who exists and is actively working in creation and events.

GOD'S ATTRIBUTES

When people consider what God is like, they tend to think of Him in human terms. Does God have a gender, male or female? Is God forgiving or judgmental? Is God a conservative or liberal in His political outlook or does He side with a particular viewpoint? There are many opinions on what God is like and who He favors. As parents, we must make sure that our voice is heard regarding the true character and nature of God, as outlined in scripture, and not based on subjective opinion.

God is all-powerful, all-knowing, and all-present. There are no limitations on God's ability. There isn't anything that God doesn't know already or that He has yet to learn. His knowledge is infinite; He knows the present, past and future. God is a spirit, all-present and not bound by time or space. "The eyes of the Lord are everywhere, keeping watch on the wicked and good" (Proverbs 15:3). God is not an inferior god that we can control, nor is He a genie in a bottle granting our every wish. We cannot shape God into our image. God is more powerful, more knowledgeable, and far superior to mankind. As Job exclaimed, "How great is God—beyond our understanding!" (Job 36:26).

God's character is described as holy, righteous, just, sovereign, unchangeable, and wise. God is holy (Psalm 99:9), flawless and without sin, and consequently all of His actions are righteous and wise. In God's perfect nature, He is fully just in His judgments; injustice is not possible with God. Further, we are assured by God that He will never change (Malachi 3:6). When God gave mankind His laws, commands, and precepts, they were given by a holy, righteous, just, and unchangeable God. Not only has God created everything, He is also sovereign and rules over His creation. While He has given man responsibility in creation, He has not abdicated His throne or authority. God expects and demands obedience to His perfect laws.

God is loving, merciful, and faithful. This love has been shown not only in His constant provision for us, but also in sending His son as a sacrifice to cover our sins, so that relationship with Him can be restored. Because of God's great love, He is also merciful. Even when we have strayed from God, He is quick to show forgiveness when we repent and welcome us back into fellowship. God is faithful to the extreme. We can be totally confident, that if God says He will do something that it will come to pass. God never lies to or misleads us. These attributes of God are sometimes misunderstood and used in the context of permissiveness where sin is concerned. Often you will hear the argument that since God is love we should be accepting of people, and by inference, also their actions. However, these attributes of God do not stand alone. Love, mercy and faithfulness are exercised in harmony with God's righteousness, which is intolerant of sin.

These attributes only begin to describe God; many more attributes are outlined in scripture. We have an amazing, capable, and powerful God. His character is perfect and beyond reproach. In light of God's attributes, it is both undeserved and remarkable that He cares so deeply for mankind, desiring to know and fellowship with each of us individually. God's amazing holy character and attributes should elicit a response from each of us of praise, worship, appreciation, and reciprocal love.

MOSES' LEGACY: A SECURE DWELLING PLACE

There is nothing more comforting than a safe place. A place where we can rest secure from danger. A place from which we can launch our dreams and be secure in the love and care of those around us. God desires to be that place for us, our "dwelling place throughout all generations" (Psalm 90:1). A dwelling place is our home, where we belong and live. It is familiar and contains the things that are important to us, a secure refuge from the world around us.

Long ago, there was a baby boy born to a Hebrew family that lived in Egypt (Exodus 2:1-10). Everything about the world that this little boy, Moses, was born into was the opposite of safe and secure. During the time he was born, an edict had been issued to kill all male Hebrew babies in an attempt to control the growing Israelite population in Egypt. Rather than kill her child, Moses' mother decided to hide him in a papyrus basket and place him in the river, hardly a safe place for a newborn. His sister watched from a distance until he was discovered by the Pharaoh's daughter. The Pharaoh's daughter had pity on this little Hebrew boy and adopted him, thus sparing his life. Moses' sister ran up to the royal princess and offered a suggestion for a nursemaid to help care for the baby. By God's grace and his sister's quick thinking, Moses' mother was chosen for the job.

As Moses grew, he was aware of his Hebrew roots. The Bible doesn't say how he became aware of this. Perhaps his nursemaid and birth mother mentioned it when she was caring for him as a young child or perhaps the Pharaoh's daughter and his adoption mother told him the story of how she found him. Regardless of how he learned this, he felt a kinship with the Hebrew people and often went out to watch them at their hard labor. One day he witnessed a Hebrew who was being beaten, and in his effort to protect the slave, he killed an Egyptian. News soon got out about his crime and Moses had to flee Egypt to avoid punishment and the death penalty. Many years passed and Moses married a woman from Midian, an area on the northeast shore of the Red Sea. While tending his father-in-law's sheep, he noticed a bush at the foot of Mount Horeb that appeared to be burning but was not consumed by the fire. As he stared at the bush, God spoke and told Moses to return to Egypt to free the Hebrew people from bondage. Despite his concerns, Moses obeyed God.

So, what does this have to do with God being a dwelling place for generations? A dwelling place is more than a physical location, it is God living in us. It is an internal faith in God's power and ability to lead, protect, and provide for each of us. Somewhere along Moses' journey in life, he had come to understand the great power of God and His attributes. Later, this internal faith would sustain Moses through the arduous task of leading the Israelites out of Egypt and the ensuing journey to return to their homeland, a physical dwelling place promised by God. Just as his mother had trusted God to protect and deliver her son, Moses trusted God to overcome unsurmountable odds to deliver and provide for the Israelites. The depth of his love and devotion to God could be seen in his song of praise, "Great and marvelous are Your deeds, Lord God Almighty. Just and true are Your ways, King of the nations" (Revelation 15:3).

EVERY MINUTE MATTERS

None of us know how much time we will have with our children. Like many parents, I remember that when my children were born, I visualized their future. I looked forward to their birth and all the things they would learn in their first year. I looked forward to their first tooth, first step, first word, and a host of other 'firsts'. I anticipated their toddler years culminating in their first day of school. Early years would speed by and soon I would face those trying teenage years. Of course, I was confident that I would be the one parent who could have a warm understanding relationship with my teen during those years. I expected my child to graduate from high school, possibly college, and eventually marriage. Yes, like so many parents, I looked forward to the passing of days and milestones with my precious child.

But suppose something happened that cut our time, mine and my child's time together short. In the life of Moses, his parents knew their time was limited from the day of his birth. As a nursemaid, Moses' mother would only have a few years with her son. In other scriptures, we read about Daniel who was ripped from his home and birthplace when he was a teen and taken to Babylon to become a servant to King Nebuchadnezzar (Daniel 1:3-6). Daniel's parents would never see their son again. We also read about Joseph; whose jealous brothers sold him into slavery as a young boy (Genesis 37:28). Joseph's father would not see his son again for several decades.

Life is unpredictable. Every day matters. We may have a lifetime to pass on knowledge about God or we may only have a short time. However, even if we cannot predict how much time we will have, we can live each day making wise decisions and taking every opportunity to teach our children the important lessons of life. How would you prioritize the truths that you teach your children about God? Where would you begin? What would be the most important moral and spiritual lessons to focus on first?

We must tell our children that God exists and can be known by His attributes that set Him apart from creation.

JOSEPH'S LEGACY: SLAVERY AND DELIVERANCE

Joseph was a favored son in his family. The youngest of 11 brothers, his dad showed preferential attention to his young son. He gave him a beautiful coat and kept him close to the house, while his brothers worked in the field. One day his brothers, filled with jealousy and anger, hatched a plan to sell him to slave traders and pretend he had been attacked by wild animals to cover up his disappearance.

Now you might think the transition from favorite son to slave would mar Joseph for life, but this was not the case. His father's lessons about God had been firmly planted in his early years. In the midst of suffering and humbling circumstances, he would remember these lessons. He would remember his father's gentle correction and godly values. These lessons would follow Joseph to Egypt and define his future path and legacy.

Even in slavery, God showed favor toward Joseph. Soon he was placed in the service of the captain of the guard, Potiphar. Everything Joseph did prospered. His master was very pleased and gave Joseph a great deal of responsibility. Unfortunately for Joseph, the master's wife also noticed his success and good looks and became attracted to him. Joseph had a right heart before God and rejected Potiphar's wife because he knew adultery would be immoral and it would be an offense to his master. He had learned the commandments of God as a young child and now, when tested, he held firm. When Joseph rebuffed her advances, she was angry and lied to her husband that he had tried to seduce her. Potiphar threw Joseph in jail, an unjust punishment. Despite this, Joseph continued to trust God.

God did not forget Joseph. In jail, once again God showed favor to Joseph. Recognizing the integrity of Joseph, soon the guards were trusting him and put him in charge of the prisoners. One prisoner told him a dream. God enabled Joseph to interpret it correctly. Later when the Pharaoh had a dream, the man remembered Joseph and called him to interpret it. When he told Pharaoh what his dream meant, Pharaoh recognized him as a man filled with the spirit of God. Joseph soon advanced out of prison and became second in command in the kingdom.

Later Joseph would save his family during a drought that affected the land. When asked by his brothers why he saved them after they had sold him into slavery, he responded "it was to save lives that God sent me ahead of you" (Genesis 45:5). What a perspective! He never forgot God and God never forgot him. Lessons from an early age not only saved Joseph, but it saved his family and a future nation.

Prayer: Lord, open our eyes that we may see how great and wonderful You are. As we grow in faith, help us to pass on the knowledge and reverence of God to future generations, that they too may recognize Your holiness and live for You. May Your name be praised forever. Amen

Reflections and Personal Study

Reflect on the main topics covered in the lesson.
Read and meditate on supporting scriptures.
Consider how this applies to your personal life.

Topic: You must be intentional about sharing your faith and beliefs with your family.

Scripture: Read Isaiah 43:10-11. How are children of God described? What is our purpose?

Belief in God
Topic: Fundamental to believing in God is the core faith that God exists.

Scripture: Read Psalm 19:1-2, Psalm 40:5, and Ecclesiastes 3:11. What are some of the ways in which we know God exists?

God's Attributes
Topic: We have an amazing, capable, and powerful God. His character is perfect and beyond reproach.

Application: List 2-3 attributes of God. Why is it important that we tell others about God's character and ability?

Moses' Legacy

Topic: Moses found a dwelling place in God that sustained him in the arduous task of leading the Israelites out of Egypt and the ensuing journey to return to their homeland.

Scripture: Read Exodus 2:1-10. How did Moses' mother display faith in her actions to protect her infant son?

Application: In Psalm 90:1, God is described as our dwelling place. This truth is not altered by circumstances in life. How has God been a dwelling place in your life?

Every Minute Matters

Topic: We need to tell our children that God exists and describe His character, teach God's will for us as expressed in His law, and show the right way to respond to God.

Application: In teaching children about God, how would you prioritize the lessons? Is one lesson more important than another?

Joseph's Legacy

Topic: He never forgot God and God never forgot him.

Scripture: Joseph was sold into slavery when he was a teen. There were many times when Joseph could have felt sorry for himself in the years that followed, but instead Joseph kept his eyes on God. Read Genesis 45:5. What was Joseph's perspective on the suffering he had endured?

Application: How have the lessons you've learned regarding God shaped your perspective on the events and circumstances you are placed in?

We do not segment our lives, giving some time to God, some to our business or schooling, while keeping parts to ourselves. The idea is to live all of our lives in the presence of God, under the authority of God, and for the honor and glory of God. That is what the Christian life is all about.

~ Robert C. Sproul
Theologian and Pastor,
Founder of Ligonier Ministries, 1939-2017

4

A LEGACY OF PRAISE AND FAITH

*These commandments that I give you today are to be on
your hearts. Impress them on your children. Talk about
them when you sit at home and when you walk along
the road, when you lie down and when you get up.*
— Deuteronomy 6:6-7

M Y CHILDREN GREW MUCH FASTER THAN I EVER
expected. In the blink of an eye they went from cuddling
in my arms as young children to adults with their own
families. As the years passed by, I had the privilege to get to know my
children as individuals with unique personalities and gifts. Together
we formed binding relationships, leading to trust, love, support and
understanding.

In our last chapter, we started with the knowledge that God
exists and we began to understand the nature of God by looking
at His attributes and character. As we grow in our knowledge of a
majestic and loving God, this should elicit a response. We respond
with worship and praise as we stand in awe of God's holiness and
works. Then as God dwells in our hearts and we draw nearer to God,
we trust Him to act on our behalf and we respond with faith, hope
and a lifetime relationship of walking with Him.

WORSHIP

Often when I think of worship, I associate it with the organized gathering and classes that are typically held on Sunday. These activities may include music, a special message or sharing the gospel, prayer, sacraments such as baptism and communion, and Sunday School classes. While these all may be a form of worship, they really don't capture the heart and spirit of worship.

The fourth commandment is "Remember the Sabbath day by keeping it holy" (Exodus 20:8). The Sabbath for the Israelites was the last day of the Jewish week, Saturday, and primarily a day of rest (Deuteronomy 5:12-14). "For in six days the Lord made the heavens and the earth, the sea, and all that is in them, but he rested on the seventh day. Therefore, the Lord blessed the Sabbath day and made it holy" (Exodus 20:11). All the other days of the week were available for work and other commitments. Keeping this commandment did not mean the Sabbath was the designated day for worship. Rather, the purpose of the Sabbath was to be a sign between the Israelites and God for "generations to come," so that they would know the Lord and understand it was the Lord who made them holy (Exodus 31:13).

The tabernacle was set up as a sacred place of worship and offerings. While there are some scriptures pointing to a sacred assembly being held on the Sabbath (Leviticus 23:3) and Sabbath offerings (Numbers 28:9), assemblies, sacrifices, teaching, and tabernacle activities occurred every day of the week. Early Christians met and worshiped together often and on various days. Later, the first day of the Jewish week, Sunday, was designated as the primary day for Christians to meet and worship, as a nod to the day of the week that Jesus rose from the dead. Meeting on Sunday, instead of Saturday, was not considered a breach of the fourth commandment to keep the Sabbath holy. Scriptures such as Romans 14:5, "one person considers one day more sacred than another; another considers every day alike," gave Christians freedom to observe a special day or to observe every day as special when it came to worship.

It is not the day of the week, place, format, or activities that define worship, but rather our attitude and righteous response to God's holiness. In the Old and New Testaments, the words most often translated to worship were in Hebrew **shachah** and in Greek *proscuneo*. These words connote a posture of being prostrate before God, either by bowing down or falling flat on the ground, in reverence and adoration. Both words capture the superiority of the Creator in comparison to mankind, the created, and mankind's subservience.

In other scriptures we find the spirit and motivation of worship. In Romans 12, we worship by offering ourselves sacrificially, putting God's will above our own, with a mind toward obedience and righteous living to please Him.

> Therefore, I urge you, brothers and sisters, in view of God's mercy, to offer your bodies as a living sacrifice, holy and pleasing to God—this is your true and proper worship. Do not conform to the pattern of this world, but be transformed by the renewing of your mind. Then you will be able to test and approve what God's will is—His good, pleasing and perfect will. (Romans 12:1-2)

Worship should also be reverent, recognizing the power and holiness of God. "Therefore, since we are receiving a kingdom that cannot be shaken, let us be thankful, and so worship God acceptably with reverence and awe, for our God is a consuming fire" (Hebrews 12:28-29). Our response to God's holiness (Psalm 99:5), power (Hebrews 12:29), mercy (Romans 12:1), goodness, and love (2 Chronicles 7:3) is to bow before Him, praise Him, adore, and love Him. To worship God in truth and spirit (John 4:23) is to recognize who God is and what He does and to respond in a spirit of humility and gratitude.

Worship serves as a reset to our thoughts, actions, and spirit, reminding us of our place in this great universe and who is in control. It refocuses our hearts and minds to revere God more than the world around us. It inspires us to walk in faith and obedience. Yes, worship is a critical lesson to teach our children, as it is with our heart, mind and body, that we are to love God fully, engaging and wholeheartedly committing our entire being to Him (Mark 12:30).

PRAISE

It was so exciting to watch our children excel at sports or other activities while growing. Whenever they would score a winning goal, play their instruments on the field or stage, make an "A", or simply draw a cute picture, it was soon the center of conversation. Perhaps we didn't sing their praises from the rooftops, but we called the grandparents, told our friends, and anyone else who would listen. Praise and excitement were the expression of our approval and pleasure.

> Praise the Lord. Praise God in His sanctuary; praise Him in His mighty heavens. Praise Him for His acts of power; praise Him for His surpassing greatness. Praise Him with the sounding of the trumpet, praise Him with the harp and lyre, praise Him with timbrel and dancing, praise Him with the strings and pipe, praise Him with the clash of cymbals, praise Him with resounding cymbals. Let everything that has breath praise the Lord. (Psalm 150:1-6)

In Psalm 150, we get a glimpse of where, why, and how we praise God. We worship Him in the sanctuary and His mighty heavens; in other words, anywhere that God is present. We praise Him for His acts of power and His surpassing greatness; in other words, for all that He is and all that He does. We praise Him with instruments; in other words, with celebration and enthusiasm. The Hebrew words translated as praise, *yadah* and *halal*, refer to an extension of hands or use of hymns in revering, giving thanks and worshiping God. There is a sense of genuine excitement as we praise God and just like the praise we give our children, the praise we give God is enthusiastic, joyful, and maybe even noisy!

Praising God is a part of our worship and a form of expression. It is also part of making God known, telling others about His goodness and faithfulness, recounting His works, and expressing appreciation for His mercy and justice. We are encouraged to praise God continually (Hebrews 13:15), an ongoing act of acknowledging God in our lives, an act that will be everlasting (1 Chronicles 29:10-11).

THE FUNDAMENTALS OF FAITH

Faith is essential to our relationship with God. As it says in Hebrews 11:6, "without faith it is impossible to please God, because anyone who comes to Him must believe that He exists and that He rewards those who earnestly seek Him."

I've often wondered how we teach faith. Unlike many things we teach our children, the exercise of faith varies with each individual. There is not just one way to have faith, but rather it is a conviction of the heart and mind that is expressed through action.

One way we might teach what it means to be faithful to God is to first be an example of living in faith. Just as Paul exhorted Timothy, "set an example for the believers in speech, in conduct, in love, in faith and in purity" (1 Timothy 4:12), we become role models to our children. Second, we can provide scriptural examples of faith. There are numerous examples given—Abraham, King David, Noah, Daniel, and many more. And third, we can discuss the essential characteristics of faith.

When it comes to faith, the number one teacher is setting an example. In the first chapter, I recounted the time when Abraham went up the mountain with his young son Isaac to offer him as a sacrifice to God. When his son questioned him, "Where is the lamb for the burnt offering?" (Genesis 22:7), Abraham calmly replied that God would provide the sacrifice. As it came time to offer the sacrifice, Abraham began to bind his son on the altar. Never do we read in the scripture that Isaac screamed out or even fought to escape. Isaac trusted his father and his father trusted God. Abraham obeyed God and lived out his faith by his actions, thus providing a real-time example for his son (James 2:21). Faith is trusting God absolutely and obeying even when we don't understand.

An individual's faith in God is shown when we are certain about God and His characteristics, obey God's commands, trust God's plan for our lives, and believe God's promises. This is why a good understanding of God's word is important to developing faith. The Hebrew word for faith, *emunah*[1], at its root refers to something or someone that is firm in their actions. While we often think of faith as a state of knowing God, it is more accurately interpreted as our resolute action emerging from our knowledge of God. In Habakkuk 2:4, we read "the righteous person will live by His faithfulness."

The essential exercise of faith involves belief, knowledge of God's word, and action. It is by exercising faith that we grow in faith. Just as a muscle is strengthened by use and exerting its capabilities to the full extent, our faith is strengthened when it is applied and challenged.

HOPE IN A SURE THING

When all the news seems to be negative, when all around us we see broken homes and broken families, when corruption is more the norm than the exception, that is when hope seems most elusive. Yet, God's holy word has been written to provide revelation, truth and direction, so that we might have endurance and be encouraged, culminating in life-changing unwavering "hope" (Romans 15:4).

Merriam-Webster defines hope as "desire with anticipation" and wanting "something to happen or be true"[2]. But the English definition of hope is not the same hope the Bible is talking about. Hope in God is more than desire and more than wishing something would be true or happen. When we find hope in the Bible, it is rooted in knowing God's word is true. It is anchored in a faith that is based on a sure thing. It is the expectation that a faithful God will indeed keep His word. How else can we "give the reason for the hope we have" (1 Peter 3:15), if it is not sure and true?

We are teaching our children about hope that is different from the one found in the world. In the Old Testament, one of the Hebrew words translated as "hope" is *yachal*. We find this word in Psalm 31:24, "Be strong and take heart, all you who hope in the Lord." This word's primary root suggests waiting patiently and trusting. It is not a hope of wishful thinking, but one established in truth.

How do we teach this type of hope to our children? Hope begins with faith, and faith begins with God's Word. In Hebrews 11:1 the scriptures teach that "faith is confidence in what we hope for and assurance about what we do not see." Faith and hope are closely related. While faith is action based on God's word being true and factual, hope is looking to the future and anticipating its fulfillment. "Hope that is seen is no hope at all" (Romans 8:24).

Since Jesus has risen from the dead and paid the penalty for our sins, we have assurance that we will receive an inheritance as children of God (Colossians 1:12). We hope for Jesus' return (Titus 2:13) confidently knowing it will happen. We look forward to being with Jesus for eternity and resurrected from the dead (John 14:19). "We have this hope as an anchor for the soul, firm and secure" (Hebrews 6:19).

DANIEL'S LEGACY: A DECISION TO OBEY THE ONE TRUE GOD

In the scriptures, we meet Daniel, whose family lived in Jerusalem. Daniel was from a royal family or at least of noble birth (Daniel 1:3). As a teen, he was handsome, well informed, and showing a high aptitude for learning (Daniel 1:4). Like all Jewish boys at this time in history, part of Daniel's education was spent at the temple learning about God, the Torah and the history of his people. As a nobleman, his other education likely included current events, etiquette, history, writing, science, and all of the skillsets necessary for a future leader.

While we don't hear about Daniel's parents in the Bible, we can assume they must have also been noble in birth. His parents likely took an active role in raising Daniel. According to the American Bible Society, during this century "the Hebrews regarded children as a gift from God and a great amount of energy was given to educating them for the future. Parents were responsible for their conduct and were the primary teachers,"[3] especially the father. Also, many of the religious traditions and festivals served to teach Daniel, and other children during this time, about his rich legacy as a nation. "Passover, the Feast of Weeks, and the Festival of Tabernacles provided opportunities for children to ask questions and to learn."[4]

As Daniel's parents raised him, little did they know what the years ahead held for them. They would only have a few short years to impress on Daniel some very important lessons. Before long, Jerusalem was captured and Daniel was whisked off to Babylon as a captive to serve the Babylonian king. He would live the remainder of his life in a strange country with strange beliefs. His parents would never see Daniel again. They would never again be able to speak a word of encouragement, love, teaching, or even correction.

Once in Babylon, Daniel distinguished himself among the boys taken into captivity. Unlike many of his peers, Daniel held to the principals and values of his faith. His first test was in the food he ate (Daniel 1:8). Later he would be tested in his tenacity and willingness to adhere to spiritual disciplines, such as meditating on the teachings of the Torah and the prophets, praying, trusting God, and obedience. Values planted early in his life would shape his future. His decision to obey God's laws and be true to those values molded his character as a man of faith. Daniel was "highly esteemed" (Daniel 10:11) by God and because Daniel made the decision to set his "mind to gain understanding" and "to humble" himself before God (verse 12), his prayers were heard by God on behalf of the people of Israel.

In faith, Daniel remembered the words of the prophet Jeremiah and believed God's promise to return the Israelites to the land promised to their forefathers after seventy years of captivity. He prayed fervently for his people, for repentance, and for restoration to their relationship with God and to their land. The seed of faith planted early in Daniel's life grew deeper throughout his life, as he lived a life of obedience, remembered his God, continued to study His word, and prayed daily.

WALKING WITH GOD

The best way to characterize an individual's walk with God is by their behavior and priorities. Some basic practices that help us know what is righteous behavior and to incorporate this into our lives are studying God's word, prayer and fellowship with other believers.

God's word is essential to the Christian walk. The Bible teaches that scripture comes from God and is useful for "teaching, rebuking, correcting and training in righteousness" (2 Timothy 3:16-17), so that the servant of God will be equipped for every good work. To incorporate scripture in our lives, we apply a similar approach to how we learn topics at school. We listen to teachers, read materials, study, memorize and ponder God's word. To truly learn God's word, we have to spend time in the Bible. Of all the ways we deepen our knowledge, osmosis (unconscious assimilation) is not one of them. Learning God's word takes effort, intentionality, and discipline.

Once we learn God's word, we should obey it. Jesus said that "those who love Him would obey Him" (John 14:23). Obedience is evidence of our heart conviction toward God. As parents, we teach obedience through example, talking to our children, and correction. As it says in Psalm 78, God "commanded our ancestors to teach their children, so the next generation would know [God's statutes], even the children yet to be born, and they in turn would tell their children. Then they would put their trust in God and would not forget His deeds but would keep His commands" (verses 5-7). This ensures the well-being of our children, as keeping the commands of God leads to blessing and walking in accordance with God's perfect plan.

With God's word and obedience, we exercise discipline of the mind, body, and soul. With prayer, we exercise the discipline of relationship. Prayer is more than telling our needs to God. It is more than a "hail Mary" pass when we get in trouble, in the hopes a merciful God will rescue us. Prayer is more than repetition and mindless phrases. Prayer is both intensely personal and relational. It is the practice of talking to God and listening to His response. While God's response is sometimes verbal as recorded in the scriptures, more often God's response is through His Word, spiritual promptings, wisdom, or guiding us to opportunities and away from destructive paths. We must learn to listen to and discern God's response. Teach your children to pray to God "continually" (1 Thessalonians 5:17), at night and through the day. Teach them to stop and listen to God. Teach them an attitude of reverence before God and anticipation of God's response. The Bible says that prayers of a righteous man are heard by God. "The prayer of a righteous person is powerful and effective" (James 5:16).

Fellowship is spending time and building relationships with other believers. In the church we talk about the body of believers. We learn in 1 Corinthians 12, that we were all "baptized" into Jesus, were given the same Spirit and now form one body (verse 13). As we continue in chapter 12, we learn that each member of the body has a different purpose, but that we are all co-dependent on one another, and together with our different abilities build each other up. Together we witness Christ's love to the world around us, showing compassion and serving one another. As parents, we introduce our children to the fellowship of believers by bringing them to worship services, Sunday School, church events, and service opportunities. As our children grow older, we encourage them to discover their place in the body of Christ and how God has shaped them with unique abilities and gifts, to serve Him.

We can be confident as we strengthen our walk with God through His word, prayer, and fellowship that God will complete the good work He has started in us, "until the day of Christ Jesus" (Philippians 1:6).

SEEDS OF KNOWING GOD AND FAITH

In Deuteronomy 6, we are instructed to teach God's commandments to our children, with the promise of a long life (verses 1-2). We are to make an impression on them as to their importance. We are to discuss them in a variety of circumstances so that our children will understand how to apply God's word to their lives (verse 7). We are to place reminders around our children to keep God's commands at the forefront of their thoughts and actions (verses 8-9). By doing these things, we are planting seeds of knowing and obeying God that will bear fruit for generations.

Prayer: Lord, we lift up our families before Your throne and ask that each individual will grow in their faith and walk near to You, obeying Your ways, all the days of their lives. Humble our hearts and minds before You so that we can worship You in spirit and truth. I pray our hope and future will rest securely in Your hands. Amen.

Reflections and Personal Study

Reflect on the main topics covered in the lesson.
Read and meditate on supporting scriptures.
Consider how this applies to your personal life.

Worship

Topic: It is not the day of the week, place, or activities that define worship, but rather our attitude and righteous response to God's holiness.

Scripture: Read Exodus 20:8. What is the command on the Sabbath? Is it necessary to worship God on the Sabbath?

Scripture: Read Romans 12:1, Hebrews 12:28, and John 4:23. What should our attitude look like in worship?

Application: Is there more than one way to worship God? How do you worship God?

Praise

Topic: The praise we give God is enthusiastic, joyful, and maybe even noisy!

Scripture: Read Psalm 150. What does this scripture reveal about where, why, and how we praise God?

The Fundamentals of Faith

Topic: An individual's faith in God is shown when we are certain about God and His characteristics, obey God's commands, trust God's plan for our lives, and believe God's promises

Application: Read Hebrews 11:6. Why is faith essential to pleasing God?

Hope in a Sure Thing

Topic: Biblical hope is anchored in a faith that is based on a sure thing.

Scripture: Read 1 Peter 3:15. Why can we give a reason for our hope in God? How is hope in God different than hope found in worldly things?

Scripture: Read Hebrews 11:1. How are faith and hope related?

Daniel's Legacy

Topic: Daniel's decision to obey God's laws and be true to those values molded his character as a man of faith.

Application: As a teen, Daniel was separated from his family and country. The values and teachings embedded into his early years would have to endure many challenges to his faith. What are some of the examples in which Daniel overcame tests to his faith and godly living?

Walking with God

Topic: An individual's walk with God is characterized by their behavior and priorities.

Scripture: Read 2 Timothy 3:16, John 14:23, 1 Thessalonians 5:16-17, and 1 Corinthians 12:13. Why are studying God's word, obedience, prayer, and fellowship beneficial to walking with God?

Seeds of Knowing God and Faith

Scripture: Read Deuteronomy 6:6-7. How do we plant seeds of knowing and obeying God into the lives of our children?

The greatest legacy one can pass on to one's children and grandchildren is not money or other material things accumulated in one's life, but rather a legacy of character and faith.

~ Billy Graham
American Evangelist, 1918-2018

5

A LEGACY OF LOVING RELATIONSHIPS

He answered, "Love the Lord your God with
all your heart and with all your soul and with
all your strength and with all your mind';
and, 'Love your neighbor as yourself."
—Luke 10:27

BACK IN THE 1960'S, A POPULAR SINGING GROUP, THE Beatles, released a ballad, "Love is all you need". It was no mystery that this struck such a chord with listeners around the world and quickly became a hit. Love is something we all desire and hope for in relationships. The teachings of Jesus almost two millennium earlier had enlightened His followers to the true meaning of love and its expression. When asked "what must I do to inherit eternal life?" (Luke 10:25), Jesus summarized all of God's commands to two things: love God and love your neighbor (verse 27).

As we covered in previous chapters, loving God begins with knowing God and then expressing that love through worship, praise, faith, hope, and walking with God. We cannot love God without knowing in our heart and mind that He exists. We might be attracted to the idea of God or even respect what He stands for, but love by its very nature is relational and until we recognize God's existence, we cannot love the being who is God, the great "I am". Once we know God and begin to understand His attributes, our response to God's existence and holiness is evidence of a heart-felt and sincere conviction and love for Him.

Love is also shown in how we treat our neighbor. Our neighbor may be our family, those who live physically near us, those we work or worship with, or even those we come across in our daily lives. Often when we think of love, we think of the feelings and commitment we have toward family and friends. While feeling or emoting is a part of love, it is not the full expression of it. When the Bible speaks of loving others, it seldom speaks of the emotion of love, but generally points to the actions which demonstrate love. Infatuation and romance are short lived, but genuine love-in-action prevails through challenges, trials, and even opposition. True love has an enduring and lasting quality, consistent and unshakeable, transforming both the recipients and the giver.

In the Bible, the word "love" is often shown as a verb, something we do, and is expressed by our actions and living in a righteous manner. It is shown in how we treat others, such as kindness and mercy. It may be shown in abstaining from harmful actions, such as murder and stealing. It can be shown in caring for the helpless, providing shelter for the homeless, feeding the poor, nursing the sick, or other actions of compassion and mercy.

Love is relational and expressed in our relationships with our family, friends, neighbors, co-workers, and a host of other relationships. Love is exercised, tested, and strengthened through our interactions with these individuals when we show self-control, subdue our anger, restrain our sexual desires, and submit to those in authority. Finally, love is both a response to how God has treated us and a reflection of His attributes in us as we show forgiveness, mercy, compassion, and other expressions of goodness, such as kindness and patience.

The Bible provides guidelines as to what we should be intentional about doing and those things we should avoid. These guidelines not only help us to stay on a path that pleases God, but they mold us into individuals of righteous and loving character.

LOVE FAMILY AND OTHERS

A family is a great place to learn how to love each other. There is a transparency in families that is often not seen in other relationships. In a family you see each other's strengths and weaknesses. You know when someone is vulnerable, got into trouble at school, is lacking skills in an area, or has a secret. You know who to call for expertise in a family, the one who is good with money or the one who can fix just about anything. This transparency sets the stage for genuine expression, not influenced by an image or pretense of perfection. It allows love to be shown in a type of purity, accepting others as they really are, with both their strengths and flaws.

Love was a choice we made in our family regardless of circumstance or behavior. For the most part, love was practiced with kindness and respect, though there were occasional lapses when family members would suddenly lash out at each other. These occasional interruptions to family harmony were generally followed with apologies, forgiveness, and soon a rekindling of bonds. While the dynamics in every family are unique, most families share a unity that endures and overcomes many challenges.

In the New Testament, the Greek words most often translated as love are *agape* and *phileo*. *Agape* refers to unconditional love and *phileo* refers to brotherly love or love between friends. In 1 Corinthians 13, Paul helps us to understand what unconditional love looks like. "Love is patient, love is kind. It does not envy, it does not boast, it is not proud. It does not dishonor others, it is not self-seeking, it is not easily angered, it keeps no record of wrongs. Love does not delight in evil but rejoices with the truth. It always protects, always trusts, always hopes, always perseveres" (verses 4-7). This unconditional love is one-sided with no conditions; nothing is expected in return.

It is with other Christians and friends that we exercise the *phileo* type of love. There are many 'one another' verses in scripture, which explain how we interact as a body of believers. Some examples are to love one another (John 13:34), help one another, be kind to and forgive one another (Ephesians 4:32), serve one another (Galatians 6:2), show hospitality toward one another (1 Peter 4:9), and edify and exhort one another in faith (1 Thessalonians 5:11; Hebrews 10:25). Brotherly love always builds others up and avoids judging, speaking evil of, lying to (Romans 14:13; Colossians 3:9; James 4:11) or in any way tearing down relationships. This type of love forms a commitment and leads to a oneness in spirit and purpose.

Unconditional and brotherly love overlook a mountain of imperfections. However, it is important for us to understand that love, in any form, does not promote or encourage sinful behavior. In loving others, we should not infer that the application of love means we should ignore and tolerate sin. Nothing can be further from the truth. There is a difference between forgiveness of sin and permitting sin. Sin always harms people, whereas love does no harm, so the objectives and outcome of the two behaviors are inconsistent with one another.

FRIENDS AND RELATIONSHIPS

The company we keep affects us in so many ways in life. The friends we choose impact our opinions, the activities we are involved in, and those associations may even affect other's opinions of us. The wisdom of choosing a path that avoids sin is summed up in Psalm 1, "Blessed is the one who does not walk in step with the wicked or stand in the way that sinners take or sit in the company of mockers, but whose delight is in the law of the Lord, and who meditates on His law day and night" (verses 1-2).

In simple application, your friends and relationships matter. We often convince ourselves that keeping company with those who live in sin will work out and we will have a positive influence on them. More likely, however, we are the ones who are influenced, and not for good, but to follow in sinful activities, immoral thoughts, and eventually a disregard for God's ways. The Bible teaches us that becoming close friends and forming bonds with sinners is not a wise decision. Now this does not mean we should be a snob and avoid anyone who disagrees with us. Jesus went to sinners and brought them salvation and hope. Many of the sinners He spoke with left their immorality and turned to God. Consider Psalm 1 again, where godly men and women are exhorted to not "walk in step with", "stand in the way" and "sit in the company" of sinners. When it comes to avoiding the company of sinners, the issue is when we keep company with evil men, hang out and adopt their values. As Paul said, "Bad company corrupts good character" (1 Corinthians 15:33).

Instead, we should have regular fellowship with people who try to follow God's law and do good to others. Seeking friends and relationships with individuals who love God reinforce our values and provide a support structure in times of trial and temptation. They encourage us to seek God and to spend time doing those things which please God. We should "encourage one another daily, as long as it is called 'Today,' so that none of you may be hardened by sin's deceitfulness" (Hebrews 3:13).

WHEN LOVE IS DIFFICULT

Love sounds easy in theory, but is often difficult to apply. Unfortunately, none of us are born with a perfect loving heart. This is a behavior that is both learned and the result of an internal transformation. It is when we submit to God and let Him rule our heart, that we are changed. The work of God through the Holy Spirit transforms us from individuals controlled by our sins into individuals who love God and love others.

Sometimes love is complicated. For example, a rebellious and disobedient child may be challenging to love. There may be conflict in relationships, disagreements, or misunderstandings. It is not always easy to love someone that is mistreating others or cruel. In each of these situations and others, we often find ourselves on our knees in prayer, seeking wisdom from God. I don't pretend to have all the answers. Over the years I have found a reliable path to guide my actions when love isn't easy: prayer, time in God's word, patience, and a watchful eye looking for an opportunity to improve the relationship. God has always been faithful to hear my prayers and guide my steps.

SELF-CONTROL

Loving others is shown in how we treat each other, recognizing God's value of each individual. If you love someone, you will respect them and your actions will be for their good, not their harm. One way to show love is through the boundaries we place on our own behavior, such as in our dress, speech, and actions. Boundaries are shown in laws which govern our behavior as a society. Boundaries also are put in place to control other's actions toward us, what we let into our lives and those things we shut out.

One of the boundaries we exercise on our own behavior is self-control, where we manage our actions and thoughts, in consideration of both the present and future. We resist the temptation to live for the moment, gratify our impulses, let others influence us without constraint, be impatient, or react compulsively.

Suppose a man is walking down the street and sees an attractive woman. He decides he wants her and in an impulsive act grabs her and forces himself on her. Is that right? Suppose a person walks into a grocery store and thinks to themselves, "I'm really craving something good tonight." He or she fills their shopping cart with ice cream, cookies, a few quick microwave meals and all the foods they desire. Then the person goes home and gorges on the food in one sitting. Is that good for one's body?

With both of these examples, it's easy to see that self-control would have been the right choice. Yet every day we are faced with choices where we can act impulsively or with self-control. Let's be honest, sometimes self-control is not the easiest path. Basically, when we live by impulse and immediate gratification, we may experience temporary pleasure but at the same time we run the risk of making ourselves vulnerable for an attack.

Perhaps "attack" is an overstatement, but if we consider where a lack of self-control might lead us it may not be far from the truth. Proverbs 25:28 says that a person who lacks self-control is "like a city whose walls are broken through." This proverb points out the vulnerability of a city with broken walls and compares this to a person who lacks self-control. A city with no walls has no protection and loses control over who or what gains access across its borders. It is vulnerable to attack from unfriendly armies or dangerous animals.

How are we vulnerable when we lack self-control? In the example above, overeating can lead to obesity and health issues. Physical, sexual, or emotional abuse of individuals destroys trust and the stability of a culture. Bad financial decisions can lead to poverty or a life of dependency. The bottom line is that self-control is essential to caring for oneself, others, and building a stable future.

The importance of self-control must have been on Paul's mind when he wrote to Titus, a fellow believer who supervised the church in Crete, Greece. In Titus 2, Paul advises Titus in the lessons he should teach various members in his church. Virtually everyone must learn self-control along with other behaviors. Self-control is not reserved just for young men and women, but is also an important quality for older men and women to apply. Paul sums up the importance of controlling one's behavior and actions as enabling men and women of faith to "set an example . . . and show integrity, seriousness and soundness of speech that cannot be condemned" (verses 7-8).

The lack of self-control causes us to be ineffective and unproductive. If we act inappropriately, we can make mistakes leading to costly corrections and rework, damage our reputation, create barriers in relationships, and hurt others or ourselves. We should be thoughtful, stop, and consider an action before moving forward. Discourage impulsive actions which can lead to trouble. Exercise self-control and boundaries by considering God's perspective and thinking through how our actions might affect others.

SEXUAL PURITY

Another Greek word which is translated to love is *eros*, which refers to sexual love. Sexual love is not a sin when carried out in the context of marriage and according to the precepts of the Bible, but it can become a sin when exercised in the wrong context. The removal of boundaries when it comes to sex may be the greatest deception of the 21st century. Many people have come to believe that adultery, fornication, homosexuality, and other perverse sexual endeavors are their personal choice and do not harm anyone. In an attempt to be accepting and non-judgmental, the prevailing social norm is to be silent as friends and family continue in sexual immorality and become desensitized to the sinfulness of this behavior.

Rooted in the Ten Commandments, the basic command from God is to not commit adultery, which is to have sexual relations outside of marriage. Simply put, God intended sex to be between a man and woman in the context of marriage. Sex in any other context, such as fornication or adultery, sex with unmarried people, or sex with someone other than your spouse is sin. In Leviticus 18, Moses made it clear that adultery not only includes sex outside of marriage but it also encompasses all sexual deviations, including sex with family members, children, neighbors, and members of the same sex.

Jesus also talked about this sensitive subject. He went even further to say that lust (Matthew 5:28), the seed of sexual immorality in our mind, is just as sinful as the actual act. This makes us reconsider the pornography of the mind – dirty jokes, dirty movies, sexually provocative songs and videos, and so forth, realizing that often our sinful actions proceed from the filth of our minds.

Sexual immorality has many victims: the individual, their partner, and society. You may think that I am overstating the impact of this sin, but the scripture teaches that God will punish those who are sexually immoral (1 Thessalonians 4:3-6), that adultery destroys individuals (Proverbs 6:32), that it leads to suffering (Revelation 2:20-22), and that adulterous individuals will not inherit the kingdom of God (1 Corinthians 6:9-10). There have been a number of sexual predators that have made the national news, such as Harvey Weinstein, Jeffrey Epstein, various national leaders, sports heroes, and even leaders in the church. The deviate nature of their abuse and manipulation of young women and men was shocking. They not only did evil in God's eyes but they affected their victims for a lifetime, emotionally and in some cases physically.

When people are sexually immoral, they not only disobey God but they harm others. This disobedience creates a wedge in our relationship with God and keeps us from knowing Him fully. It breaks down families and the structure needed for a healthy and growing society. Sexual immorality devalues individuals by making them instruments of base desire, instead of seeing them as God sees them, a person created with both value and purpose.

SUBMISSION

In biblical times, submission was understood to be a part of life. The concept of submitting one's own will to the authority or will of another is found throughout the scriptures. We submit to human authority, such as kings and governors (1 Peter 2:13-14), to elders (1 Peter 5:5), to parents (Ephesians 6:1; Colossians 3:20), to spouses (1 Peter 3:1, 7) and to each other out of respect (1 Peter 2:17). Submission is more than cultural; it is necessary for society to flourish. A lack of submission to authorities results in chaos, anarchy, and in some cases physical and mental harm. A lack of submission to others creates an attitude of self-importance and selfishness.

Submission is not an abdication of oneself. It doesn't mean that we are no longer unique individuals living out a life using our God-given gifts and abilities. It is not slavery or a forced servitude by another. Submission is a decision, not coercion, to place your will and plans in subjugation to another. The Greek word for submit is *hupotasso*, which means to subordinate, obey, be subject to and to submit oneself to.[5]

Not only should we submit to authority and others, we also

submit to God. Consider James 4:7, "Submit yourselves, then, to God." In other translations, this act is made clearer with words like "surrender" (Contemporary English version), "give yourselves humbly" (The Living Bible), and "place yourselves under God's authority" (God's Word translation). We place our will on the altar before God, choosing to submit ourselves to God's holy and perfect will.

Submission is a necessary attitude to maintain order and to have harmony in relationships. For example, in the human body there are various parts, each with its specific function. The brain directs each part to accomplish the objective for the whole body. Each part must be submissive, fulfilling its role, to have order and harmony. If the foot decided to be the hand, or the ear decided to be an eye, it would hinder the end goal. Further, there can only be one brain or director. In using this analogy for the church, Paul concluded "God has put the body together, giving greater honor to the parts that lacked it, so that there should be no division in the body, but that its parts should have equal concern for each other" (1 Corinthians 12:24-25).

Teaching our children submission begins at an early age, when we place boundaries around their activities and behavior, exercising parental authority and expecting obedience. Children need to understand that even as adults, they never fully outgrow submission. It may look different than it did when we were children, but there will always be someone in authority over us or someone we choose to submit to out of deference and respect.

RUTH'S LEGACY: MOTIVATED BY LOVE

What started as an adventure brimming with hope and opportunity had become a heart-breaking memory. Years earlier, Naomi's family had relocated to the country of Moab to find work and escape the famine in Judah. Everything seemed to be headed in the right direction when things began to change. First, Naomi's husband died and then ten years later her sons died as well, leaving Naomi alone with her daughters-in-law (Ruth 1:3-5).

More than ever, Naomi felt the sting of being a stranger in the land with no other relatives. Soon she made the decision to return to her home in Bethlehem. As she set out on the road, she told her daughters-in-law to go back to their families and find new husbands. At first, they resisted, until one of them, Orpah, left. The other daughter-in-law, Ruth, refused to leave Naomi, reconfirming her commitment and bond (Ruth 1:16-17). Unable to convince her to leave, together the two women made the long journey.

As they arrived in Bethlehem, Naomi guided them to her former house. There was much work to be done to restore the home and find food and water. Ruth busied herself caring for Naomi, proving her love with every step and chore. Naomi guided Ruth to the field of a relative, where she was allowed to glean anything left by the harvesters. Both family and neighbors could see Ruth's commitment to Naomi and respected her actions (Ruth 2:11-12).

Eventually, Ruth married again and had a child, Obed. Having endured many hard years, Naomi once again found a smile as she held her grandson, on her lap. Then the women said of Naomi, "Praise be to the Lord, who this day has not left you without a kinsman-redeemer. . . for your daughter-in-law, who loves you and who is better to you than seven sons, has given him birth" (Ruth 4:14-15).

Even though Ruth was a foreigner and from a nation that worshiped idols, she understood what it meant to love another person and sacrifice for them. She grew in her commitment to Naomi and proved her love by leaving her home, caring for Naomi, and submitting to her directions once in Bethlehem. Her love was an example to many and respected by those who saw it. Ruth later would become the grandmother to a future king, David, and be one of the few women listed in the genealogy of Jesus (Matthew 1:5).

DeLinda N. Baker

FORGIVENESS, MERCY, AND COMPASSION

When I think of America, I think of a nation that has been generous to its neighbors both locally and abroad. There is no shortage of good works that have been done for others: food banks, clothing donations, medical provisions and aid for third world countries, donations of time and materials to help our neighbors recover from natural disasters, and many more good works are part of our culture. While there are many good people with good hearts in this country, there are also individuals who simply go through the motions of doing good works for appearance sake or to have a deduction on their taxes.

It is satisfying to point to our good works, which can be seen by others as praiseworthy and noble, that suggest a good character but don't necessarily require it. In a parable, Jesus described the Pharisees as "whitewashed tombs, which look beautiful on the outside but on the inside are full of the bones of the dead and everything unclean" (Matthew 23:27). In Texas, we refer to this type of individual as "all-hat", but "no cattle". In other words, someone who has all the appearance of being a cowboy, but is not one in reality.

When it comes to settling differences, we also see actions taken for the sake of appearance versus being genuinely inspired by heart-felt motivation. It is easier to go through the motions of having resolved an issue, without actually letting go of it on the inside. Our natural tendency is to hold grudges, get even, defend our rights and reputation, and hate our enemies. It is more satisfying to retaliate, resent, and ignore someone than it is to actually forgive them. Yet, forgiveness is what we are called to do. In forgiving others, we show compassion and mercy, forego judgment, and replace it with love. It is an action proceeding from a thankful, forgiven, and changed heart.

Where would we be without forgiveness? The Bible teaches that all men have sinned and are undeserving before God (Romans 3:23). If God had not forgiven each of us, we would be in a terrible place deserving God's judgment and unable to do enough good works to offset our sin. Instead, God in His mercy chose to send His Son to reconcile the penalty for our sins, give His own life as a sacrifice, and usher in forgiveness to our lives. It is truly freeing to not get what you deserve. Just like any criminal who is given the opportunity for a do-over in life, we rush forward with gratitude and a fresh outlook.

God has asked His children to resemble Him in this matter and to forgive, be merciful and show compassion in the same way He has shown it to us. "Bear with each other and forgive one another if any of you has a grievance against someone. Forgive as the Lord forgave you" (Colossians 3:13). We are asked to be longsuffering and patient and to forgive those who persecute and wrong us (Romans 12:14). "Administer true justice; show mercy and compassion to one another" (Zechariah 7:9). We are encouraged to have mercy and refrain from rushing to give people what they deserve (Luke 6:36). In this matter, God calls us to the humility of recognizing our own shortcomings as we deal with others. We are no better than our neighbor and should treat them as we hope God and others will treat us (Matthew 7:12).

I recall a news story where a police woman in Texas was convicted to a jail sentence of ten years for shooting her neighbor. Of course, she claimed it was an accident, but the jurors determined it was still manslaughter and deserved a penalty. As she was emotionally processing the judgment she had just received, she appeared to be going through a slew of emotions. She was distressed that she was going to jail, but at the same time she was relieved that she did not receive a life sentence. Her regret and repentance were apparent. The brother of the deceased man stepped forward and hugged her, and then he told her that he forgave her. The judge in the case was later criticized for her response to this woman's grief, not because of a lenient sentence, but because the judge also showed compassion. To the surprise of many, she stepped down from her bench and put her arms around the sentenced woman and gave her a Bible[6].

We don't know yet how these acts of compassion will affect this woman over the weeks and years to follow while she serves her sentence, but both the brother and the judge chose forgiveness, mercy, and compassion. The scriptures teach us that forgiveness is very powerful. It doesn't always remove the consequence of our actions, but it gives life both to the giver and recipient. Let us teach our children the power of forgiveness both by example and deed. Truly, "mercy triumphs over judgment" (James 2:13).

ANGER

Anger is pervasive in society today. It is not enough to disagree with decisions made by the leaders of our society, to be disturbed by injustices, or to have debate on issues, but today it is increasingly commonplace to see individuals respond with anger. Those who disagree with us are perceived as our enemies. There is little room in relationships for compromise and discussion. This social indignation pervades our relationships, business deals, and social norms. With seeing so much anger in the faces of my neighbors and leaders, I found myself asking if anger is the response that God wants and expects of us? Is showing anger in conflict with showing forgiveness?

In the Bible we learn that there is an appropriate role for righteous anger. When people do horrible evil things to others, are unjust, or deceptive it is right to be angry. When individuals are hypocritical in worship, feign righteous acts, or disrespect God's holiness it is right to be angry. In expressing righteous anger, we agree with God on those things which oppose His law, show disrespect to His divine and holy nature, or are unfair in the treatment of others.

In fact, we read in scripture that God is angry when men disobey Him or attack His people. An example of this was Jesus in the temple (Matthew 21:12-13). One day as He came to worship, He saw all of the tables in the courtyard surrounding the temple where foreign currency was exchanged for Hebrew coins and animals were sold for sacrifice. A bustling business had emerged at the doorsteps of the house of worship, but the men involved in the trades were corrupt and in fact a "den of robbers". Upon seeing this corruption on the doorsteps of where people came to worship God, Jesus was angry and overturned the tables, exposing their evil intentions.

God also shows anger when men disobey Him. After escaping

Egypt, the Israelites wandered in the wilderness for 40 years as a result of their disobedience. The Lord's anger burned because "the whole generation ... had done evil in His sight" (Numbers 32:13). Later during the time of Joshua's leadership, again the Lord chastised His people for refusing to give up their evil practices and stubborn ways (Judges 2:19-20).

There is also inappropriate anger. We should not harbor anger at those who do us wrong, but rather we should forgive them and pray for them. "Love your enemies and pray for those who persecute you" (Matthew 5:44). We should not be angry at those who differ with us and are sincerely trying to do the right thing. Instead we are exhorted to be patient and carefully consider our words. Also, we should not be angry when God corrects us. God corrects those He loves (Proverbs 3:12) and never corrects individuals unfairly.

Finally, anger should not consume our emotions. We shouldn't rush to anger, but instead be "slow to speak" and "become angry" (James 1:19). The scripture warns us that uncontrolled anger can lead to sin and unrighteousness.

> Be still before the Lord and wait patiently for Him; do not fret when people succeed in their ways, when they carry out their wicked schemes. Refrain from anger and turn from wrath; do not fret—it leads only to evil. (Psalm 37:7-8)

Instead of being angry, the scriptures encourage patience, discernment, compassion, and mercy. The next time you feel yourself becoming angry, take a deep breath and allow your anger to give way to mercy and forgiveness (Micah 7:18).

JOHN'S LEGACY: LOVE RECEIVED AND GIVEN

In the area of the Sea of Galilee there was an ordinary man, named John, who caught fish for a living, along with his brother and father. He didn't have a formal education, but had grown up in the Jewish culture, aware of the traditions and teachings of the temple. Now that Rome had expanded its territories, the presence of soldiers was an everyday sight. So far, the soldiers had not kept the Jewish population from worshiping nor had they hindered their daily work and activities. It was an uneasy occupation by a foreign government that seemed to be more interested in power and expansion than extinction of a population.

It was in this environment that a godly man, Jesus, emerged with a message of salvation, restoration, and hope. One day this teacher and prophet began to call his disciples. He saw John and his brother James by the seashore fishing and called, "Come, follow Me" (Matthew 4:19). The brothers, aware of this man's reputation, eagerly dropped their nets and joined Jesus. Ten other disciples were called by Jesus, varying in education and profession, but sharing the commitment to His teachings and obedient to their faith (Acts 14:22).

As John faithfully followed Jesus and learned from His teachings, John often shared in his gospel that he felt loved by Jesus. When he sat reclining next to Jesus (John 13:23), was standing next to Jesus' mother at the foot of the cross (John 19:26), and when he spotted the resurrected Jesus on the seashore (John 21:7), John referred to himself as the "disciple whom Jesus loved." John had formed a relationship with Jesus deeper than just that of a follower; Jesus made him feel valued and loved.

John reciprocated this love by accepting the responsibility to care for Jesus' mother after His crucifixion, by faithfully obeying Jesus' command to make disciples of men (Matthew 28:19-20), and by teaching and caring for Jesus' followers. In his three letters to Christians in the area around Asia Minor, John taught the followers of Christ that love was proven by obedience, love for others, and compassion (1 John 2:5; 4:7-8, 21; 5:2-3).

As he grew old, John never seemed to tire of serving God. The last letter in the New Testament records the vision John was given of heaven and the coming judgment. Humbly he calls himself a servant, faithfully testifying to all that he saw, and anxiously awaiting Jesus' return (Revelation 1:1, 22:20). From the time John first answered

Jesus' call to follow him until his death many years later, John both experienced Jesus' love for him and reciprocated by showing his love for Jesus through obedient and faithful service.

THE GIFTS OF GOODNESS

As men and women of faith, we are ambassadors of God. The testing of our commitment to God and the truth of our conviction are born out in action. In addition to the many ways of showing love that we've already discussed, there is an opportunity to reflect God in performing good deeds to our neighbors and treating them in a way that shows respect and worth. This is a very important part of our witness in the world. As we testify to a loving God who offers salvation and hope, we confirm God's love for the sinner by being loving ourselves.

Each day there are many opportunities for us to be a light in a dark world, standing out with our acts of love. As God's chosen people, we clothe ourselves with "compassion, kindness, humility, gentleness, and patience" (Colossians 3:12). We can open our pocketbooks and give generously to those in need, respond with a kind word, help our neighbors, comfort a hurting friend, and more.

These actions, along with other spiritual fruits (Galatians 5:22-23) such as keeping peace, showing goodness, and faithfulness, are an outpouring of a heart committed to God and form the foundation for the positive actions and feelings that we express to others. For example, we can choose to patient when an error is made or someone may be slow to learn a concept, forgiving instead of getting angry, and faithful to keep our word.

At the end of the day, our attitude toward others is proven by our actions. "Let us not love with words or speech but with actions and in truth" (1 John 3:18)

DeLinda N. Baker

A LIFE OF LOVE

Even as we set our course to please God, we are told, "Whoever pursues righteousness and love finds life, prosperity and honor" (Proverbs 21:21). Like the apostle John, our relationship with God begins by being the recipient of God's great love. Love transforms us and soon we find ourselves becoming agents of love, giving freely to others just as we have received. How exciting that the end of this journey of love is a full, blessed, and holy life.

Prayer: O Lord, how can we express our gratitude for the perfect love You have shown us? Show us the breadth of Your love for each of us that is wider, longer, higher, and deeper than we can possibly know or grasp (Ephesians 3:18). We pray that we will be changed by Your love and be faithful to love others as You have loved us. Thank you, Lord, for Your many mercies. In Jesus name we pray, Amen.

Reflections and Personal Study

Reflect on the main topics covered in the chapter.
Read and meditate on supporting scriptures.
Consider how this applies to your personal life.

Topic: Jesus boiled down all of God's commands to two things: love God and love your neighbor.

Love Family and Others
Topic: True love has an enduring and lasting quality, consistent and unshakeable, transforming both the recipient and the giver.

Scripture: Read 1 Corinthians 13:4-7. What does unconditional love look like?

Application: What is the objective of brotherly love? How is it shown?

Friends and Relationships
Topic: Seeking friends and relationships with individuals who love God reinforce our values and provide a support structure in times of trial and temptation.

Scripture: Read Psalm 1:1-2. How would you describe what it means to keep company with sinners? Does this mean we should avoid sinners altogether?

When Love is Difficult

Topic: Love sounds easy in theory, but is often difficult to apply.

Application: In your experience, when has it been difficult to love someone?

Self-Control

Topic: Self-Control is when we manage our actions and thoughts, in consideration of both the present and future.

Scripture: Read Proverbs 25:28. How does a lack of self-control make a person vulnerable?

Sexual Purity

Topic: Sexual immorality devalues individuals by making them instruments of base desire.

Application: Do sexual sins harm ourselves? Do they harm others?

Submission

Topic: Submission is a decision, not coercion, to place your will and plans in subjugation to another.

Application: Why is submission an important aspect in relationships?

Ruth's Legacy
Topic: Both family and neighbors could see Ruth's commitment to Naomi and respected her actions.

Application: How did Ruth show her love to Naomi?

Forgiveness, Mercy, and Compassion
Topic: In forgiving others, we show compassion and mercy, forego judgment, and replace it with love.

Scripture: Read Colossians 3:13, Zechariah 7:9, and James 2:13. How do forgiveness, mercy, and justice work together?

Anger
Topic: Uncontrolled anger can lead to sin and unrighteousness.

Application: When is anger appropriate? When is it inappropriate?

Application: What can we do instead of being angry?

John's Legacy
Topic: John felt loved by Jesus and reciprocated by caring for His mother, faithfully spreading the Gospel, and caring for Jesus' followers.

The Gifts of Goodness
Topic: These actions are an outpouring of a heart committed to God and form the foundation for the positive actions and feelings that we express to others.

Scripture: Read Colossians 3:12. What are ways we can perform good deeds for our neighbors? Should we expect anything in return?

A Life of Love

Scripture: Read Proverbs 21:21. What does a righteous and loving life lead to?

We are either in the process of resisting God's truth or in the process of being shaped and molded by his truth.

~ Charles Stanley
Pastor, Founder of In Touch Ministries, 1939-today

6

A LEGACY OF RIGHTEOUS LIVING

*You, however, must teach what is
appropriate to sound doctrine.*
— Titus 2:1

EVERY DAY WE ARE FACED WITH DECISIONS. DURING my professional career, I remember many times when I had to make a choice of doing the right thing, the wrong thing, or doing nothing at all. It wasn't always easy or even a clear-cut decision, sometimes complicated by complex circumstances and peer pressure. In the end, after careful and final consideration, those decisions would either impress management or diminish my performance and professional progress.

The choices we make in life have a way of steering our paths in one direction or another. Even abstaining from action, making a choice to do nothing, or making a choice that is somewhat neutral, sets the stage for the future. Every choice we make has the potential to impact ourselves and others, for good or evil.

When Jesus was speaking with the crowds at the Sermon on the Mount, He taught them many lessons about righteous behavior. He talked about adultery and divorce, murder and the desire to get even with those who wronged us, giving to the needy, what we should treasure in life, and more. He talked about those very issues that people have dealt with for centuries and still encounter today and every day. In the midst of the wide-ranging topics, He cautioned His followers to "enter through the narrow gate" (Matthew 7:13). "For wide is the gate and broad is the road that leads to destruction, and many enter through it. But small is the gate and narrow the road that leads to life, and only a few find it" (Matthew 7:13-14). Why the sudden warning? It was as though Jesus sensed a common thread between the topics He was covering and felt a need to caution His listeners that a serious, potentially life threatening, decision lay before them.

Jesus did not specify what criteria defined a gate as narrow or wide, but if we look at the context of His other messages related to righteous living, one way to understand the "narrow gate" is in keeping God's law and having a right heart toward others. The scriptures teach us right from wrong, placing restrictions and boundaries on our choices, effectively narrowing the gate. Finding this path requires study, seeking the truth in God's word, application, and correction. Following the narrow path is not always easy, but calls upon each of us to make thoughtful choices in life: to obey the law of God, to discern right from wrong, to make the best choices versus marginal ones, to treat others with good not evil, and to consider the long-term impact.

Of course, it would be much easier to choose the wide gate, which has fewer restrictions. There may be elements of good works, noble intentions, or even thoughtful consideration in going down the wide path. Choosing the wide gate does not mean an overt disregard of everything that is good, but rather it is a matter of subservience, a decision to follow man versus God. In choosing the wide gate, where anything goes or where right is defined however a person chooses, destruction follows as individuals disregard or compromise God's boundaries. We need to remember that there is only one way, God's way, to eternal life. Jesus claimed unequivocally, "I am the way and the truth and the life. No one comes to the Father except through Me" (John 14:6).

Titus 2 further emphasizes why it is important to turn toward the narrow path. It is the grace of God and the promise of salvation that motivates us to say "No" to "ungodliness and worldly passions" (verse 12). We choose to live "self-controlled, upright and godly lives" (verse 12), understanding that Jesus died on the cross in order to "redeem us from all wickedness" and "to purify for Himself a people that are His very own, eager to do what is good" (verse 14). After God has paid such an enormous price, to live any other way would marginalize His sacrifice.

The decision to do right or wrong has long-term spiritual consequences leading to life or destruction. The Bible teaches us that a righteous man is blessed by God, but a sinful man is cursed (Proverbs 3:33). A righteous man has fellowship with God (Psalm 23), but a sinful man is separated from God (Isaiah 59:2). A righteous man bears much fruit, but a sinful man is blown away and soon forgotten (Psalm 1:3-4). Choosing a righteous life is an important decision and one that we must each make.

In the sections that follow we'll take a closer look at some of the life issues that Jesus talked about and the choices we can make to turn toward the narrow path. We'll look at what it means to love each other and the heart attitudes that lead to murder, stealing, greed, and lies. We must teach the way to righteousness if we are to guide future generations on a path that leads to God and life.

CHOOSE LOVE NOT HARM

In the previous chapter we discussed loving relationships. When we base our actions in love, the result is harmony and well-being. God did not create us to hurt one another. In Romans 13, Paul reminds fellow believers that "love does no harm to a neighbor . . . therefore, love is the fulfillment of the law" (verse 10). When we sin by harming our neighbor, we are failing to reflect God's goodness. In Leviticus 19, we are exhorted "Be holy because I, the Lord your God, am holy" (verse 2). As God's children, we should strive instead to live lives that reflect God's image and exhibit attributes consistent with

God's character: qualities like love, kindness, mercy, faithfulness, gentleness, and justice.

The root source of harming others is a heart that is inclined toward evil. "For it is from within, out of a person's heart, that evil thoughts come—sexual immorality, theft, murder, adultery, greed, malice, deceit, lewdness, envy, slander, arrogance and folly" (Mark 7:21-22). With God's help we are able to overcome these sinful tendencies and to do the right thing toward others. Instead of harming others, our goal should be to build one another up and encourage others to obey God. "Each of us should please our neighbors for their good, to build them up" (Romans 15:2).

CHOOSE TRUSTING GOD OVER MURDER

When it comes to the topic of murder, this seems an action so violent and reprehensible that only the worst in society or possibly the mentally ill would be capable of it. The average well-balanced individual might even consider themselves above such an action. I remember my shock a few years back when I heard on the news that a man had murdered his wife. Not long after that, it was reported a woman had murdered her four young children. How could this be? How could someone in a trusted relationship turn against their family and murder the very people with whom they had spent so many years together, in family gatherings, exchanging gifts, and sharing goals.

Usually when we talk about murder, we focus on the action and circumstances surrounding the deed. The Bible offers some insight into murder, qualifying actions that are and are not murder, and looking at the heart of the perpetrator. Murder has to do with taking a life with stealth, having an evil motive, and unjustly carrying out the crime against a neighbor. Killing enemies in war, taking a life as a punishment for heinous crimes, and accidental acts that lead to a death are not considered to be murder in the scriptures.

When Jesus first talked about murder on the Sermon on the

Mount, His focus was the heart of the individuals. Murder has its root in uncontrolled anger, hatred, and disrespect toward others. It might be expressed through name calling, "raca" meaning empty-headed or stupid or "fool."

> You have heard that it was said to the people long ago, "You shall not murder, and anyone who murders will be subject to judgment." But I tell you that anyone who is angry with a brother or sister will be subject to judgment. Again, anyone who says to a brother or sister, "Raca," is answerable to the court. And anyone who says, "You fool!" will be in danger of the fire of hell. (Matthew 5:21-22)

These early stages of anger were as unacceptable to God as their most violent expression of murder, since they showed an evil heart intent on tearing down and devaluing another person.

The first murder recorded in the Bible was Cain murdering his brother Abel in Genesis 4:8. The recounting of this event began with an act of worship, that of sacrificing part of one's livelihood to God, an offering. Though we don't read about the circumstances leading up to the sacrifice, sinful acts seldom appear suddenly. Instead, over time, one sin leads to another, frustration builds, and compromises are made, until the full expression and sinful action occurs.

In this case, Abel brought an offering of cattle, placing a portion of the firstborn of his flocks before God. Cain brought an offering of some of the fruits from the soil before God. In making their offering, God looked upon the hearts of the two men. The Bible says that God accepted Abel's offering, but not Cain's. This had nothing to do with whether the type of offering was animal or harvest, but had everything to do with the attitude of the men and their actions outside of worship. Later we find out in the New Testament that "by faith Abel brought God a better offering than Cain did" (Hebrews 11:4) and that Cain's "actions were evil and his brother's were righteous" (1 John 3:12).

God chastised Abel and he became angry at God for rejecting his offering. God reminded Cain that it was his choice to sin. "If you do what is right, will you not be accepted? But if you do not do what is right, sin is crouching at your door; it desires to have you, but you must rule over it" (Genesis 4:7). Instead of repenting, Cain let this anger marinate in his heart, leading up to his lashing out and murdering his brother, an individual approved by God.

There is much anger and hate in our world today. As you watch nations shouting insults and threats, you wonder if there is a path to peace. As you watch the politics of our own nation, accusations and distortions of facts, you wonder if there is a path to reconciliation. As you watch families and marriages breaking down and turning against one another, you wonder if there is a path to love. Anger and hate never lead to acts approved by God, but this is only possible through a changed heart that chooses a path of righteousness and trusting God.

In the previous chapter, we talked about letting go of anger and responding instead with forgiveness and mercy. As individuals who trust God, we do not need to worry about getting even or seeking vengeance when we are wronged. Instead, Jesus encouraged alternative responses of turning the cheek and generosity, doing good instead of evil, and a willingness to forgive.

> You have heard that it was said, "Eye for eye, and tooth for tooth." But I tell you, do not resist an evil person. If anyone slaps you on the right cheek, turn to them the other cheek also. And if anyone wants to sue you and take your shirt, hand over your coat as well. If anyone forces you to go one mile, go with them two miles. Give to the one who asks you, and do not turn away from the one who wants to borrow from you. (Matthew 5:38-41)

Now this is not to say that we should put ourselves at physical or emotional risk, but rather it is instead a response of willing submission, compassion and longsuffering. Instead of retaliating when we are injured, we offer the "other cheek" and trust vengeance to God. Instead of seeking justice when we are wronged, we forgive and are patient and longsuffering. Instead of holding back from those wanting something from us, we respond with generosity. We do all these things for the sake of the gospel and the opportunity to share God's love. After all, Jesus has done all of these things for us. He has willingly suffered, forgiven, loved, and generously given of Himself to those who repent and follow Him.

A heart trusting in God to provide our needs and bring justice is the ultimate cure to the anger in this world. When we let go of our anger, we make room for love. When we allow God to vindicate us, we make room for mercy and forgiveness. When we love our neighbor and are willing to sacrifice our rights in lieu of getting even, we make room for God to shine through us.

CHOOSE WORK NOT STEALING

A popular movie series in the 1960's and 1970's was the **Pink Panther**. The key character of the movie was a suave sophisticated thief who charmed his way into the homes of the rich and famous and then stole valuable jewelry and artifacts from them. In the movie, stealing was shown as classy, smart, and totally forgivable, while law enforcement was portrayed as bumbling and idiotic. Now granted this was a movie, but its premise was not that far from the truth.

Today stealing is considered by some to be clever, acceptable as long as you're not caught, and a crime that may be overlooked depending on the degree of the impact. Thievery may take the form of major crimes, such as purchasing items with counterfeit money, defrauding investors, or online fraud and email phishing. Other forms of stealing may seem more benign, such as stealing supplies from your office to use at home, taking a piece of candy from a store, or taking salary for hours not worked. In every case, whether major or minor, whether caught or hidden, stealing at its heart is still the same. It is motivated by the desire to take something without paying for it or earning it and without the permission of the lawful owner.

Jesus reveals the heart of the thief as being destructive and murderous (John 10:10), in robbing its victims of the fruit of their labors and having an insatiable desire for more. Thieves are deceptive and secretive, hiding their evil deeds by the dark of night or behind closed doors.

The dishonesty of stealing may fool people, but it never fools God. When Mary, the sister of Lazarus, wiped Jesus' feet with expensive perfume (John 12:3), Judas Iscariot was critical of her saying it would have been better for her to sell the perfume and give the money to the poor. The truth was that Judas wanted the profit for himself. As keeper of the money bag for the disciples, Judas "used to help himself to what was put into it" (John 12:6). While Judas pretended to be sympathetic to the poor, in his heart he was a thief and greedy.

In addition, stealing is contrary to God's commands since it fails to show love to a neighbor and hurts its victims. They may lose something material or something personal, something major or something minor, but inevitably they lose peace of mind in knowing that a thief can rob them at any time. They no longer feel secure in their home or business. In some cases, thieves shoot their victims or physically harm them when they carry out their robbery. In other cases, a person or company may not realize they've been robbed until later, but they are still left with not only being a victim, but doubly punished since they will carry the financial burden either with extra insurance, security, or cost of replacement.

It is important that we teach our children not to steal, no matter how small the item, so that they can learn to be content and to trust God to provide all their needs. The remedy to stealing begins with a heart that trusts God, is content with His provision, and then takes the talents and abilities God has provided and uses them productively. In Ephesians 4, thieves are encouraged to stop stealing and instead to "work, doing something useful with their own hands, that they may have something to share with those in need" (verse 28). In working, possessions are obtained honestly and openly, the result of labor and investment of talents and resources. In sharing the fruits of their labor, instead of bringing forth destruction an individual gives emotional healing, hope, blessing, and opportunity to its recipients.

CHOOSE GENEROSITY NOT GREED

In the dictionary, greed is defined as "a selfish and excessive desire for more of something than is needed."[7] Consider the tenth commandment, which is dedicated to this base sin: "You shall not covet your neighbor's house. You shall not covet your neighbor's wife, or his male or female servant, his ox or donkey, or anything that belongs to your neighbor" (Exodus 20:17). Coveting hurts our neighbor and damages our relationship with God. This perpetual dissatisfaction and overwhelming desire for wealth or possessions warps our soul. We begin to think of ourselves as somehow unfulfilled, regardless of our circumstances. Having sufficient or even abundant resources does not diminish a covetous heart from wanting more. We have an obsessive desire for something or someone else, thinking it will become a source of contentment and happiness in life. In so doing, this misplaced trust effectively de-thrones the true God and makes money, possessions, and other objects of desire the new god(s) in our lives.

Giving ourselves over to desire for a neighbor's house, spouse, servant, and other possessions can lead to many sins: envy, greed, hate, stealing, and more. "You desire but do not have, so you kill. You covet but you cannot get what you want, so you quarrel and fight" (James 4:2). We must resist the temptation to dwell on what we don't have and to let dissatisfaction take root in our heart. Instead, we should turn to God with our needs and requests.

Nowhere in scripture are we taught that the abundance of possessions will make us complete or happy. In fact, often the opposite is true. An abundance of possessions and money complicate our lives and increase our responsibility and accountability to others.

"From everyone who has been given much, much will be demanded; and from the one who has been entrusted with much, much more will be asked" (Luke 12:48). With the acquisitions comes greater responsibility and a need for increased discernment to handle these things in a manner that honors God. An abundance in money or possessions are never intended for self-absorption, self-satisfaction, or hoarding. Rather, it is more appropriate to think of ourselves as stewards who have been given temporary responsibility over these possessions, to distribute, disperse, or manage them for God's glory.

An alternative to greed is generosity, a complete 180 degree turn in attitude. Instead of holding on to what we have and wanting more, we freely release the profit and even surplus of our possessions to others. "One person gives freely, yet gains even more; another withholds unduly, but comes to poverty. A generous person will prosper; whoever refreshes others will be refreshed" (Proverbs 11:24-25). Generosity without expectation of anything in return is an expression of kindness and a willingness to share, an awareness of the needs of others and taking action to help, a contribution to the church and community to benefit others, and more.

> Command those who are rich in this present world not to be arrogant nor to put their hope in wealth, which is so uncertain, but to put their hope in God, who richly provides us with everything for our enjoyment. Command them to do good, to be rich in good deeds, and to be generous and willing to share. In this way they will lay up treasure for themselves as a firm foundation for the coming age, so that they may take hold of the life that is truly life. (1 Timothy 6:17-19)

In 1 Timothy 6, Paul warns the rich to not "put their hope in wealth", but instead to "put their hope in God", to do good, and be generous (verses 17-18). The result is to avoid placing confidence in a temporary and uncertain world, but instead finding permanent treasure in a God who cannot be shaken and the real meaning of life.

CHOOSE TRUTH NOT LIES

In our family we told each other the truth, even if it wasn't what we wanted to hear. No lies were allowed. There would be greater discipline for telling a lie than for doing something that was forbidden. My hope was that this would create an environment where our children knew that what they were hearing was true and based on reality.

Truth begins with God and God's very character is based on truth. Jesus described Himself as the way, truth, and light (John 14:6). Knowing that God is truthful, and utterly incapable of lying or deceit, is very important to our ability to trust God and know that everything He stands for is reliable and trustworthy. It instills the confidence of having a foundation that is unshakeable, unchanging, and lasting. Real truth remains the same regardless of circumstances and events. It enables us to say "The Lord is trustworthy in all He promises and faithful in all He does" (Psalm 145:13).

Likewise, God wants this same characteristic to define His children. In Psalm 15, King David talks about the kind of people who will dwell with God in His sacred tent on His holy mountain. Essentially, God is looking for righteous individuals who speak the truth (verse 2). People who know these truthful individuals can depend on what they say as being correct, accurate, honest, and dependable. Being truthful is more than just presenting facts, it has to do with what we say, how we say it, and our intent when we say it. When truth is the foundation, it expresses itself through love and respect for others. There is no deceit, or manipulation, or a need to conceal anything. Everything is out in the open. Truth refuses to slander others, wrong a neighbor, break a promise, or take advantage of others (verses 3-4).

As we set out to become individuals established in truth, we learn not only to speak the truth, but to discern truth in others. In the Bible we are admonished to avoid lying, any form of mistruth or deception, and even the company of liars. Truth should be our mantra without exception. "Whoever of you loves life and desires to see many good days, keep your tongue from evil and your lips from telling lies" (Psalm 34:12-13). Not only should we avoid lying and deceit, we should also be careful not to use our words to stir up trouble through actions like gossiping, backbiting, quarreling, or foolish arguments (2 Timothy 2:14-16, 23). These ungodly activities tear apart relationships and offend God.

I remember when I was young, children used to chant "sticks and stones will break your bones, but words will never hurt you." As I've gotten older, I don't agree with that common saying any more. Words do hurt and they do serious damage. They are like a stream of water, that seems harmless in good weather, but add a few days of pouring rain and that harmless stream becomes a torrent capable of carving out gorges and destroying homes. "The words of the reckless pierce like swords" (Proverbs 12:18).

Remember that Satan is described as a "liar" and the "father of lies" (John 8:44). When we lie and deceive, we are behaving like Satan. Lying and deceit are not only sin, but they are detestable to God. Words may seem harmless, after all they are not sticks or stones, but they have the potential to lead to great harm. The Lord hates liars, so we should do everything in our power to avoid this detestable behavior and seek truth instead.

SAMUEL'S LEGACY: A CHOICE TO OBEY

Many years ago, there was a woman named Hannah who was married to a man who lived in the hill country of Ephraim. For Hannah, life was difficult. Her husband, Elkanah, had two wives. While the other wife, Peninnah, had several children, Hannah was barren. If that wasn't difficult enough, the other wife taunted her and bragged about her children. This went on year after year, and Hannah was quickly approaching the breaking point.

Now, Elkanah was a man who faithfully followed the priestly teachings. Every year he journeyed with his family from the hill country to Shiloh, to worship and sacrifice to the Lord. One year, Hannah left the family group in tears. As usual, her rival Peninnah had been provoking her about being barren. Hannah knew where to go with her sorrow and shame. She went to the temple to pray and seek comfort from God. Hannah vowed to God, "Lord Almighty, if You will only look on Your servant's misery and remember me, and not forget Your servant but give her a son, then I will give him to the Lord for all the days of his life, and no razor will ever be used on his head" (1 Samuel 1:11). The priest of the temple, Eli, saw Hannah praying. Once Eli realized she was sincere, he told her to "go in peace," trusting God to answer her prayers (1 Samuel 1:17). Hannah believed God and immediately her countenance changed. Soon Hannah became pregnant and gave birth to a son.

Once her son, Samuel, became old enough, Hannah and her husband took him to the temple where he remained (1 Samuel 1:26-28). I can't imagine how difficult it would be to leave their young son, but Elkanah and Hannah were fully committed to keeping their word and vow to the Lord. Even after leaving their son, Hannah saw him yearly and always brought him gifts. She had not stopped loving him or caring for him. By their actions, these parents were showing their son the importance of being faithful to God.

While Samuel was growing up in the temple, there were two other boys growing up with him, the two sons of Eli. As we learn in scripture, there was a stark contrast between the behavior of Samuel and Eli's sons. Eli's sons "were scoundrels" and "had no regard for the Lord" (1 Samuel 2:12). They showed disrespect for temple practices and committed adultery (1 Samuel 2:17, 22). Even though Eli warned his sons to stop sinning, he tolerated his son's actions and, in some cases, joined them in eating choice parts of the offerings sacrificed in the temple. God rebuked Eli for his actions (1 Samuel 2:29) and as a result, God said that no one in Eli's family would reach the prime of life (1 Samuel 2:32). Eli's sons were killed in battle and upon hearing the news, Eli fell back in his chair, broke his neck, and died. Even though the family was born into a priestly line, their opportunity to serve God in this capacity was taken away.

In contrast, Samuel grew "in stature and in favor with the Lord and with people" (1 Samuel 2:26). He understood the importance of following God's laws and respecting the temple. His responses from childhood, "Here I am" (1 Samuel 3:4) and "Speak, for Your servant is listening" (1 Samuel 3:10), characterized his lifetime response toward God. When God revealed His plans, Samuel faithfully relayed His messages and did what the Lord said. His life was defined by listening to God and obedience. As a result, God continued to speak to Samuel and guide his actions and decisions. "All Israel from Dan to Beersheba recognized that Samuel was attested as a prophet of the LORD" (1 Samuel 3:20), who would later be directed by God to anoint the first two kings of Israel, King Saul and King David.

When we listen to God and obey, God speaks to us and guides our path. God does not speak to the rebellious or those who refuse to hear His call. This is why it is so important that we teach our children the importance of choosing to live righteous lives and obeying God.

CHOOSE WISDOM & DISCERNMENT

When it comes to making good choices, you need more than rules. For those decisions in life that aren't black and white, you need wisdom and discernment to know how to apply godly principles. I used to think wisdom automatically came with age and experience. Actually, wisdom comes from God. It is not the result of experience as much as it is the result of searching, knowing and applying God's word, and seeking understanding. God sets our feet on the path of wisdom when we turn over our wills to Him and ask for this remarkable gift (James 1:5). Then He guides us along the path that will cultivate and grow wisdom in our hearts and actions.

Some will say that you can be wise apart from God. That may be true in part, but it is different from the wisdom we obtain from God. Worldly wisdom which is rooted in mankind's experience and understanding is limited by our finite knowledge and imperfect nature. This wisdom will never be sufficient or complete. However, wisdom received from God is infinite, perfect, and good, since it comes from an all-knowing eternal God and is dependent on God's holy character.

How do we obtain this supernatural godly wisdom? Wisdom begins with submitting to the authority and sovereignty of God in our lives and acknowledging God's ways over our own. As it says in Proverbs 1:7, "the fear of the Lord is the beginning of knowledge." In trying to understand God's ways, we put forth effort to grow in both knowledge and application. Wisdom is not automatic or an overnight accomplishment; it involves intense desire and searching (Proverbs 2:3-4). Finally, obedience is not only the fruit of a wise heart, but it is the necessary condition for a continued relationship with God. True wisdom will be accompanied by a love for righteousness and discreet and guarded actions which will keep you on an upright path (Proverbs 2:20).

Whereas godly wisdom is exercised when we strive to see life from God's perspective and act accordingly, discernment is the ability to distinguish between truth and lies, right and wrong, and good and evil, particularly when they are obscure. Similar to wisdom, discernment comes from God and is fine-tuned and developed through the study of God's word. "But solid food [the word of God] is for the mature, who by constant use have trained themselves to distinguish good from evil" (Hebrews 5:14). Along with knowledge, discernment may also involve observation, understanding, and discovery.

Eleanor Roosevelt, a former First Lady of the United States, once said, "Never mistake knowledge for wisdom. One helps you make a living; the other helps you make a life." To teach our children to seek godly wisdom and to exercise discernment is a precious gift that will stay with them for life.

PRACTICE, PRACTICE, PRACTICE

To grow in maturity, we must practice making good choices and obeying God, thus gradually becoming more successful and consistent in our behavior. Living out the tenets of righteous living is not an easy course to set in life. To increase in righteousness, we must continually study, learn, practice, correct our course when we stray, and persevere in obedience to God's laws, commands, and precepts.

There are many scriptures that talk about how we should apply the scriptures to our lives and the pursuit of godly living. One of my favorites is from Paul's letter to the Corinthians.

> Do you not know that in a race all the runners run, but only one gets the prize? Run in such a way as to get the prize. Everyone who competes in the games goes into strict training. They do it to get a crown that will not last, but we do it to get a crown that will last forever. Therefore, I do not run like someone running aimlessly; I do not fight like a boxer beating the air. No, I strike a blow to my body and make it my slave so that after I have preached to others, I myself will not be disqualified for the prize. (1 Corinthians 9:24-27)

Like a runner, we have to take our spiritual training seriously if we are to be victorious. "Strict training" implies disciplined daily routines, self-control, practice, and persistence. It is hard work, not an accident or surprise. We can't be aimless in our pursuit; we have to clearly set our goals and a plan for achieving them. We can't be unclear of the enemy and "beating the air," we need a clear vision of righteousness and a clear understanding of evil and the very thing we should avoid. We must practice, test our abilities, and push ourselves to do more than we think possible.

All of this is done in faith and in the power of the Holy Spirit, enabling us to live in a way that honors God. If we choose obedience and the path of righteousness, the reward will be greater than we can imagine.

Prayer: Heavenly Father, You alone are worthy of our worship and obedience. You alone are perfect and without sin. Forgive us for our shortcomings and guide us as we walk in Your path. Help us to be faithful stewards of Your word. Show us how we can teach others Your laws and precepts and how we can pursue righteousness in our families and community. Empower us, O Lord, to live holy godly lives. In Jesus name we pray, Amen.

Reflections and Personal Study

Reflect on the main topics covered in the chapter.
Read and meditate on supporting scriptures.
Consider how this applies to your personal life.

Topic: Choosing a righteous life is an important decision and one that we must each make.

Scripture: Read Matthew 7:13-14. When Jesus talks about the choice between the wide gate versus the narrow gate, what do you think He means?

Scripture: Read Titus 2:11-14. What does the grace of God motivate us to do? Why is it important to choose a godly life?

Choose Love not Harm
Topic: When we sin by harming our neighbor, we are failing to reflect God's goodness.

Scripture: Read Romans 13:8-10 and Mark 7:21-22. How do we harm our neighbor? What does God want us to do instead?

Choose Trusting God Over Murder

Topic: Anger and hate never lead to acts approved by God, but this is only possible through a changed heart that chooses a path of righteousness and trusting God.

Scripture: Read Matthew 5:21-22. What is the underlying root cause of murder? Why would name calling be so offensive to God?

Scripture: Read Matthew 5:38-41. What is a better option than getting even with someone? Why?

Choose Work not Stealing

Topic: Jesus reveals the heart of the thief as being destructive and murderous, in robbing its victims of the fruit of their labors and having an insatiable desire for more.

Scripture: Read Ephesians 4:28. What is the remedy for stealing?

Choose Generosity not Greed

Topic: Coveting hurts our neighbor and damages our relationship with God.

Scripture: Read James 4:2. How does coveting possessions hurt our neighbor? How does it affect our relationship with God?

Scripture: Read 1 Timothy 6:17-19. What should be the motivation for generosity?

Choose Truth not Lies

Topic: God is looking for righteous individuals who speak the truth.

Scripture: Read Psalm 15. What kind of people will live on God's holy mountain?

Samuel's Legacy

Topic: Samuel understood the importance of following God's laws and respecting the temple.

Scripture: Read 1 Samuel 3:4-10. How did Samuel respond to God's call? How did God respond to Samuel?

Scripture: Read 1 Samuel 2:17-22. How did Eli's sons show disrespect for God? How did God respond to Eli's family?

Choose Wisdom & Discernment

Topic: True wisdom will be accompanied by a love for righteousness and discreet and guarded actions which will keep you on an upright path.

Application: Read Proverbs 1:7 and Proverbs 2:1-5. How do you gain wisdom?

Practice, Practice, Practice

Topic: To increase in righteousness, we must continually study, learn, practice, correct our course when we stray, and persevere.

Scripture: Read 1 Corinthians 9:24-27. Why must we practice doing the right thing? How long does it take before we stop making mistakes and live a perfect holy godly life?

God, you have made us for yourself, and our hearts are restless till they find their rest in you.

~ Saint Augustine
Christian Theologian and Author, Bishop of
Hippo Regius of North Africa, 354-434 ad

7

A LEGACY OF FULFILLMENT

I am come that they might have life, and that
they might have it more abundantly.
— John 10:10 [KJV]

WHAT IS THE SECRET TO HAPPINESS AND fulfillment? Mankind has been asking this simple question for ages. Is fulfillment found in being young, beautiful, and healthy? Is it found in a nice home or in a family, loving spouse, and children? Or is it found in a fulfilling career and mastery of skills? Fulfillment in life is so important to people, the pursuit of happiness was declared a fundamental right in the Declaration of Independence, a right to pursue joy and live in a way that makes you happy as long as you don't break any laws or violate the rights of others.

When it comes to seeking fulfillment, we are always rushing to pursue and find fulfillment on our own. The cosmetic, plastic surgery, and clothing businesses cater to our desire for physical beauty and generate millions in profits. A home and garden network on cable television fills every hour of the week promoting the satisfaction found in a perfect, renovated home. We throw ourselves into our jobs, trying to make a living and in the hopes of receiving a little affirmation of our worth. It's exhausting to exert so much energy and to still find ourselves needing to do more to be completely fulfilled.

Yet, Jesus, directs us to seek another source for fulfillment. In John 10:10, He reminds us that He is the one who has "come that they might have life, and that they might have it more abundantly." We need to remember that God, our creator, knows us better than we know ourselves. While mankind seeks many avenues to fulfillment, true fulfillment independent of circumstances and environment can only come from a relationship with God.

In this chapter, we are going to cover several aspects of fulfillment. They are not the method or tools used to find fulfillment, but rather they are the results of a fulfilled life. After all, regardless of how we pursue fulfillment, what people really want is the satisfaction and feeling of completion that come from blessing, prosperity, happiness, contentment, rest, joy, and peace.

BLESSING, PROSPERITY, AND HAPPINESS

Who would not like to be blessed, prosperous, or happy? These words bring to mind a picture-perfect life, free from conflict, where we have everything we need and maybe a little more. According to Webster, to be blessed is to enjoy "happiness" or bring "pleasure, contentment, or good fortune"[8]. When you read the scriptures, the Hebrew and Greek words have a similar meaning to their English counterpart, and are generally linked to happiness, welfare, purpose, and fulfillment. Yet, as we read scriptures that talk about blessing, it is sometimes counter-intuitive as to who receives blessing, where it is found, and what leads to it. A well-known and often read psalm, Psalm 23 gives us a glimpse of blessed individuals, people who don't lack anything, people who have everything they could possibly need (verse 1).

> The LORD is my shepherd, I lack nothing. He makes
> me lie down in green pastures, He leads me beside

quiet waters, He refreshes my soul. He guides me along the right paths for His name's sake. Even though I walk through the darkest valley, I will fear no evil, for You are with me; Your rod and Your staff, they comfort me. You prepare a table before me in the presence of my enemies. You anoint my head with oil; my cup overflows. Surely Your goodness and love will follow me all the days of my life, and I will dwell in the house of the LORD forever. (Psalm 23:1-6)

In this psalm, people are compared to sheep that are led to a calm and refreshing place by their shepherd, where they receive both physical and spiritual restoration (verses 2-3). They are comforted when they go through difficult times and elevated when others abuse them or hurt them (verse 4-5). They are loved and treated like something or someone that has value and worth. Not only are their needs met, but they are met abundantly (verse 5) and they are welcomed in the house of the Lord (verse 6). What a beautiful image and the epitome of fulfillment and satisfaction.

The recipient of this tremendous blessing, the sheep, refers to me, or rather, you. "He makes **me**," "leads **me**," "refreshes **me**," and so forth. This care and oversight are provided by the shepherd (verse 1), who is specified to be the Lord. Those receiving the refreshment, comfort, and protection in the verses that follow are fully dependent on the care and benevolence of the shepherd. It is the shepherd who chooses their path and resting place. It is the shepherd who continually provides for their needs. It is the shepherd who loves and welcomes them and, ultimately, bestows the blessings on them. The flock in the care of the shepherd belong to him and are his responsibility.

Blessing is not always found in an environment that is pleasant. As we looked more carefully at Psalm 23, the sheep who were under the care and guidance of a good Shepherd experienced good times and bad. They experienced blessing in good times: when they were in green pastures, when they were by still waters, and when they were on the right paths. They were also comforted and provided for in bad times: in the darkest valley and in the presence of their enemies.

In the Beatitudes, Jesus also talks about blessing, but not for those who are prospering, but for those who mourn, the meek, the persecuted, and those facing false accusations for His name's sake (Matthew 5:3-4,10-11). For these individuals He encourages patience and comfort in knowing they will eventually be with Him. He also talks about blessing on those doing the right thing and seeking God, those who hunger and thirst for righteousness, the merciful, the pure in heart, and the peacemakers (Matthew 5:6-9). For these individuals, He promises they will be filled, shown mercy, see God, and be recognized as His children.

How is it possible that blessing is received both in good times and bad? Blessing takes the form of many shapes: prosperity, victory, comfort, restoration, forgiveness, mercy, and other forms of undeserved love and kindness from God. Blessing can be received by those whose well-being and prosperity is easily seen by others. It can be received by those who appear to be victims and suffering. It can be received by both sinners, who are forgiven, and the righteous who are living in an upright manner. In summary, it is received by those seeking and trusting God, regardless of their circumstances.

Certainly, there will be valleys and mountaintops in life. There will be times of prosperity and times when it may be difficult to make ends meet. In all circumstances, we will be blessed if we follow the path where God leads us, trusting our benevolent shepherd to meet our every need, filling our cup until it is overflowing. "Blessed are those whose help is the God of Jacob, whose hope is in the Lord their God" (Psalm 146:5).

JOB'S LEGACY: PERSEVERANCE AND REVERENCE

When you think about contentment, Job may not be the example you would choose in scripture. He is an individual who is most famously known for his suffering and perseverance. When we first meet Job in scripture, he was a man who had it all: property, money, happy family life, and good health. His wealth was so impressive that he was described as the "greatest man among all the people of the East" (Job 1:3). Yet with all that Job had, it did not go to his head. He was "blameless and upright", fearing God and avoiding evil (Job 1:1).

The day came when Satan was roaming the earth. When he came before God, they discussed Job, a man who had walked before God faithfully. Satan questioned whether Job would be as faithful and blameless if he lost those things treasured by mankind: wealth and family. God agreed to allow Job to be tested in this fashion. Satan attacked Job and in a single day Job lost his oxen, donkeys, sheep, camels, seven sons and three daughters.

Now put yourself in Job's place. Imagine that unthinkable tragedy fell on you in a single day and that you lost all your wealth and family. It would be enough pain to lose even one of these, but to lose them all would be extremely difficult. Yet, at the end of the first chapter of Job, we see a man grieving in sorrow but refusing to sin. "In all this, Job did not sin by charging God with wrongdoing" (Job 1:22). Job's response showed humility before God and a genuine reverence.

Satan then approached God again, saying that the only reason Job was still worshipping God was that he still had his health. In essence, Satan was implying that Job was extremely self-centered. Again, God agreed to let Satan attack Job and soon Job was covered in boils. Still Job did not sin (Job 2:10), but again replied "Shall we accept good from God, and not trouble?".

Job's friends and wife were not very helpful. His wife counseled him to curse God, die, and get it over with. His friends pointed out that he must have sinned or he would not be going through such suffering. While never denying God's sovereignty and right to bring good in our lives as well as to take it away, Job did his fair share of complaining. He cursed the day of his birth (Job 3:1), despised his life (Job 7:16), and wished he was dead (Job 6:8-9). Can you identify with this level of despair?

Despite Job's suffering, he still had enough pride remaining to worry about what others thought (Job 17:2) and to remind his friends of his track record of doing the right thing before God and how he was undeserving of the suffering he was receiving (Job 27:2-6). Finally, God had enough of his self-pity and grasps at self-righteousness. God reminded Job of His sovereignty and pointed out Job's sin. Job immediately repented and God forgave him. God restored Job's relationship with Him along with Job's possessions, family, and health. "The Lord blessed the latter part of Job's life more than the former part" (Job 42:12).

But did you notice that at no point did Job ask God to restore his possessions? Job's contentment stemmed from his relationship with God, not his surroundings. Ultimately, his sin was self-righteousness, not greed. Job's willingness to accept suffering from God without giving in to the temptation to curse God proved his allegiance and commitment to God. In going through suffering, Job's understanding of God was further deepened, as shown in his profession: "my ears had heard of You but now my eyes have seen You" (Job 42:4).

Later in scripture, we see Job's legacy. Job was counted righteous, along with great patriarchs like Noah and Daniel (Ezekiel 14:14). Job's perseverance and patience in suffering became an example to those in the early church and future generations, who would share in difficult and trying circumstances (James 5:11). He would be remembered for his reverence for God and refusal to deny Him, even when he lost everything, showing that our relationship with God is more valuable than possessions.

CONTENTMENT

The secret to successful marketing is to create a need in a buyer's life for a product. It has to be implied that no matter what you already have, if you don't have this new improved item, your life will not be as complete, functional, or effective as it should be. The more successful you are in convincing someone of this perceived necessity, the more likely that individual will run out and buy the product.

People are constantly comparing themselves to others. The

phrase often used to describe this phenomenon is "keeping up with the Jones's." Questions are designed to highlight discrepancies in life, questions like is our house as big, our car as new, our job as prestigious, our children as smart and talented, and the list goes on and on. This comparison leads to a perpetual state of dissatisfaction and wanting more. It blinds us to the multitude of blessings we have already received.

So, what is the secret to contentment? As we read about Job, a man who went from having everything to having nothing, and then to having everything and more again, in the end he concluded that contentment was found in subservience to God and the acceptance of His purpose. In Job 36:11, he said "If they obey and serve Him, they will spend the rest of their days in prosperity and their years in contentment". Basically, Job was saying contentment comes from a right relationship with God.

Even though this may be contrary to what we hear in the world, contentment is never found in keeping up with the Jones, or even outdoing them. Contentment is both something we choose and a state of mind, that of feeling satisfied. Whether or not we feel contented is based on what we think, ponder and meditate on. If we dwell on what we don't have, we will find ourselves dissatisfied. Seeking contentment in money and possessions is a trap that can lead to harmful desires, ruin, and destruction (1 Timothy 6:9). Money and possessions are deceptive as security or a source of contentment, because they are temporary and unreliable. However, if we set our thoughts on God, seeking and obeying Him first, the material things of the world will seem less important. When we commit our sense of control, security, desires, and needs to God there is a stability and comfort that we experience since God has promised that He will never leave or forsake us (Hebrews 13:5). As Jesus reminded us, God already knows what we need.

> For the pagans run after all these things, and your heavenly Father knows that you need them. But seek

first His kingdom and His righteousness, and all these things will be given to you as well. (Matthew 6:32-33)

Contentment grows and finds its fullness when we trust God to provide all our needs. God is our portion and our cup (Psalm 16:5), the source of our spiritual inheritance, strength, and everything we need. The blinders fall off our eyes and we begin to realize how much we have already received and the abundant treasures that lie ahead of us.

PAUL'S LEGACY: ZEALOUS DEVOTION

Paul was a man of great passion. From the first time we meet him in scripture until his last recorded letter, he always seemed to be in the middle of all the activity. He was never a man for the sidelines. No, Paul gave one hundred percent to his beliefs, work, and fellow believers.

If Paul carried around a resume, we would see that he was a devout Pharisee from the tribe of Benjamin, intent on living a life devoted to and perfectly obedient to God. Raised in the Jewish faith, he studied under Gamaliel and excelled in his understanding of scriptures (Acts 22:3), where he would have mastered Jewish history, the Psalms, and the works of the prophets. Paul was also born a Roman citizen, which gave him certain rights, including a public hearing. Paul had the trifecta of Roman citizenship, religious family line, and education.

He followed God's laws so fervently that when he felt there was a cult that was disrespectful to God, he was in full support of its persecution and removal. Initially, Paul viewed the Christians and their church, The Way, as such a cult. Paul approved of killing Stephen (Acts 8:1) and helped with imprisoning men and women in the church in Jerusalem (Acts 8:3). He even asked for letters from the high priest so that he could imprison followers of the Christian church in a neighboring town, Damascus (Acts 9:1-2).

It was this very man, the one actively persecuting the church, that God noticed and decided would be his choice to proclaim the gospel to the Gentiles. It would not be easy to convert a man like Paul. Jesus appeared to Paul on his way to the church in Damascus, as a bright light. Jesus identified himself and then told Paul to go to the city and wait for further instructions. For three days Paul did not eat or drink, but prayed and pondered the message he received from Jesus. (After all, even though Paul was persecuting Christians, he was sincere in his devotion to the Jewish faith.) During this time God gave him visions and began to show him how much he would have to suffer in his service to God. After three days, Ananias came to him, prayed that God would restore his sight, and baptized him (Acts 9:17-18).

After his conversion, now convinced that Jesus was the Messiah and fulfillment of prophecy, Paul became as zealous in defending the Christian faith, as he had been earlier in resisting it. It would take someone who was well versed in scriptures to help lead the new church, particularly the Gentiles who had not grown up with these teachings, to show them how Jesus fulfilled the scriptures, and to guide them in the application of its truths. It would take someone with great courage to not let personal threats, trials, and jail shake his faith. It would take someone who persevered and kept his faith in the face of obstacles to be an example for fellow Christians who were also facing persecution.

His commitment was so sincere and unwavering that he endured challenging circumstances, such as persecution and imprisonment. He faced opposition from both Roman authorities and Jewish leaders. He persevered through tough times, but somehow managed to find joy, peace, and even contentment. At last, Paul shared his secret to being content despite the circumstances around him, it was simply to keep his focus on Christ. As Paul wrote in his letter, "I know what it is to be in need, and I know what it is to have plenty. I have learned the secret of being content in any and every situation, whether well fed or hungry, whether living in plenty or in want. I can do all this through Him who gives me strength" (Philippians 4:12-13). By finding his strength and contentment in Christ, despite persecution and resistance, Paul was able to faithfully persevere in serving his fellow believers.

FINDING REST

Not too long ago, I went to a museum exhibit featuring the paintings of the well-known artist, Vincent van Gogh, who lived in the late 1800's. While best known for his landscape and still-art paintings, Van Gogh loved to paint the common person at work in the field, cooking, sitting around the table and in various poses. As I looked at the people in Van Gogh's paintings, one thing that caught my attention was the way he captured the emotions of the people he painted. There was a sad, worn out, and almost melancholy expression on many of their faces. You could tell their lives were not easy and that rest and relief from worry and bondage, was hard to come by. It reminded me of the scripture "So my heart began to despair over all my toilsome labor under the sun" (Ecclesiastes 2:20).

That isn't so different from today. Even though work may be easier with the help of modern technology, life can still be difficult. Daily we work long hours, strive to take care of our families, move from one activity to another, and fill our lives with duties and obligations. Many of us find ourselves in bondage to financial needs, family concerns, peer pressure, and a number of other forms of enslavement. Like the early Israelites looking to escape their bondage in Egypt, our hearts desire to find a place where we can find rest and renewal.

We seek relief and escape from the drudgery with weekend trips and vacations, where we hope the pursuits of pleasure will refuel us to face our work with renewed energy. While this may provide some physical rest, true and enduring rest is found in a right relationship with God. This is the type of rest Jesus was talking about when He said, "Come to Me, all you who are weary and burdened, and I will give you rest" (Matthew 11:28).

This internal rest is anchored in peace and security, an eternal calm knowing that God is sovereign over the events and circumstances of this world. In Hebrews 4, we learn that the requirements for this rest are faith and obedience. "For we also have had the good news proclaimed to us . . . but the message they heard was of no value to them, because they did not share the faith of those who obeyed" (verse 2). God intends for those who have believed (verse 3) to receive this rest "today" (verse 7) and every day that our hearts are open to Him. This rest of the soul, mind, and body provide us the needed renewal for going forward in our work for God. As the psalmist proclaims, "Truly my soul finds rest in God; my salvation comes from him" (Psalm 62:1).

JOY AND PEACE

Every Christmas we sing carols expressing joy and peace. We remember the birth of Christ and how He was the harbinger of promise and peace. Many in the early church believed that the Messiah would defeat the Roman empire and usher in a new world, free from persecution and bondage. Indeed, Jesus has ushered in those things, but not in the way the Jewish people expected.

Jesus was born in a simple man's world. Similar to the images depicted by Van Gogh's paintings, Jesus was born in a common place, a manger. He was raised and lived in the home of a common man, a carpenter, who worked hard to put food on the table and provide for his family. Even as Jesus began His ministry, He did not come marching into the city with armies and strength, but He rode a donkey. Jesus understood the common man and empathized with the hard life he endured.

Jesus' message of fulfillment was one that would not be found in a plethora of possessions and physical security. The joy found in scriptures refers to an exceeding gladness and pleasure found independent of circumstances. When we look at scriptures, we discover inner lasting joy is found . . .

- in the presence of God (Psalm 16:11),
- keeping God's precepts (Psalm 19:8),
- loving righteousness (Psalm 45:7), and
- salvation (Psalm 51:2).

Does it surprise you that joy is found in loving God and being loved by Him? Is this what the world around us is teaching? The world wants you to think that joy is found in possessions and circumstances. It is true that we enjoy these things in the short term, but the joy we are talking about here is lasting and life changing.

To further emphasize this point, let us look at Romans 14. "For the kingdom of God is not a matter of eating and drinking, but of righteousness, peace and joy in the Holy Spirit, because anyone who serves Christ in this way is pleasing to God and receives human approval" (verses 17-18). It is a redefinition of joy from one that is self-serving to one that is God-focused. The unexpected irony is that the more we work to create joy for ourselves, the further we get from it. The more we look to God and seek what is right in His eyes, the more we become filled with the immeasurable and overflowing joy that we've been seeking.

Peace, or *Shalom*, refers to a blessing we receive from God, a state of prosperity, rest, safety and welfare. It is when we say "all is well" with the world and in our own lives. One verse that captures the spirit of this word is "The Lord gives strength to His people; the Lord blesses His people with peace" (Psalm 29:11).

While peace may refer to physical safety and security from enemies, it is also a state of internal well-being. In the New Testament, the Greek word *eirene* refers to an inner rest, a spirit that is no longer at war with itself or with God, but is at rest, complete and secure, independent of circumstances. "Do not be anxious about anything, but in every situation, by prayer and petition, with thanksgiving, present your requests to God. The peace [*eirene*] of God, which transcends all understanding, will guard your hearts and your minds in Christ Jesus" (Philippians 4:6-7).

This word was also used when Jesus talked about the peace He gave His followers. "Peace I leave with you; My peace I give you. I do not give to you as the world gives. Do not let your hearts be troubled and do not be afraid" (John 14:27). "I have told you these things, so that in Me you may have peace. In this world you will have trouble. But take heart! I have overcome the world" (John 16:33). This type of peace can never be taken from God's children.

Only God can satisfy our desires and make us complete. Love, joy, and peace are the fruit of an abiding and continuing relationship with God. They elevate mankind above the human elements and circumstances of this world. They are the expressions of a life well-lived, full and complete.

WHEN ENOUGH IS ENOUGH

You will know when you are fulfilled, because suddenly enough is enough. You won't need more things, better relationships, or even a pristine environment and conditions to make you complete.

We worship a God who has done more than created us. God is in our lives every day, blessing us as He patiently takes us to green pastures and still waters. He guides us along His path for us and completes the work He has started in us to make us perfect and able to live in accordance with His plan, using the gifts and talents He has given us. He gives us an abundant and full life, immeasurable joy, unshakeable peace, and perfect rest. We will not lack anything but will be given all that we need, finding contentment and satisfaction. It is a supernatural fulfillment, fueled from the power of God, an unlimited resource of treasure and boundless in possibilities.

A wise theologian from the 4th century, St. Augustine, once said "God, You have made us for Yourself, and our hearts are restless till they find their rest in You." This is what it means to be fulfilled. God is all that we need and truly is enough.

Prayer: O, Lord, may my heart find satisfaction in Your presence and provision. Show me the bountiful blessings You have placed in my life. Teach me to be content in every circumstance and unwavering in my devotion to You. Fill my heart with joy and peace and give me rest. In Jesus name I pray, Amen.

Reflections and Personal Study

Reflect on the main topics covered in the lesson.
Read and meditate on supporting scriptures.
Consider how this applies to your personal life.

Blessing, Prosperity, and Happiness

Topic: Blessing implies happiness, welfare, purpose, and fulfillment.

Scripture: Read Psalm 23:1-6. Who leads us to a place where we are secure and all our needs are met? What role do the followers have in getting there?

Application: Blessing can be received in times of prosperity and times of suffering. How is that possible?

Job's Legacy

Topic: Job's perseverance and patience in suffering became an example to those in the early church and future generations, who would share in difficult and trying circumstances.

Scripture: Read Job 42:4. What is the difference between seeing God and hearing about God?

Contentment

Topic: Contentment grows and finds its fullness when we trust God to provide all our needs.

Scripture: Read Job 36:11. What is the secret to contentment?

Scripture: Read Psalm 16:5. What does it mean for God to be our "portion"?

Paul's Legacy

Topic: Paul became as zealous in defending the Christian faith as he had been earlier in resisting it.

Scripture: For the sake of the gospel, Paul endured many trials and persecution. Read Philippians 4:12-13. How could Paul say he was content?

Finding Rest

Topic: Internal rest is anchored in peace and security, an eternal calm knowing that God is sovereign over the events and circumstances of this world.

Scripture: Read Hebrews 4:2-7. What must we do to enter into God's rest today?

Joy and Peace

Topic: Joy refers to exceeding gladness and pleasure found in the presence of God, keeping God's precepts, loving righteousness, and salvation.

Topic: Peace, or *Shalom*, refers to a blessing we receive from God, a state of prosperity, rest, safety, and welfare.

Topic: The Greek word *eirene* refers to an inner rest, a spirit that is no longer at war with itself or with God, but is at rest, complete and secure, independent of circumstances.

Application: What are the common ingredients that lead to a lasting joy and peace?

When Enough is Enough

Topic: You will know when you are fulfilled, because suddenly enough is enough.

We do the greatest service to the next generation of Christians by passing on to them undimmed and undiminished that noble concept of God that we received from our Hebrew and Christian fathers of generations past.

~ A.W. Tozer,
The Knowledge of the Holy,
Christian Author and Pastor, 1897-1963

8

A LEGACY FOR ETERNITY

*Surely the righteous will never be shaken; they will
be remembered forever. They will have no fear of bad
news; their hearts are steadfast, trusting in the Lord.
Their hearts are secure, they will have no fear; in the
end they will look in triumph on their foes. They have
freely scattered their gifts to the poor, their righteousness
endures forever; their horn will be lifted high in honor.*
— Psalm 112:6-9

THROUGHOUT THIS BOOK WE HAVE BEEN LOOKING
at how we pass our faith to the next generation, whether it be
the next generation of family members or the next generation
of believers. We have looked at those key tenants which define our
faith, in the hope that we will be more effective in communicating to
others what it means to have faith and to walk with God.

When we talk about having faith as a Christian, we are referring
to believing and trusting God. This faith starts with knowing that
God exists and recognizing His sovereignty. However, faith involves
more than just believing that God exists, it also includes what we do
in our lives as a result of that faith. Our actions which accompany
faith are evidence of our sincere conviction in God.

Faith in action is shown in how we respond to God's existence and sovereignty, through praise, worship, and prayer. It is shown in keeping God's commands and loving God and our neighbor. It is deepened and tested as we walk with God and make choices leading to a righteous life. The result of this beautiful and growing relationship is a God-given and supernatural fulfillment, regardless of our circumstances.

The importance of the legacy we leave our children is emphasized in its eternal consequence. When you stop and think about it, many men and women of faith have preceded us. Consider how the faith and obedience of men in the Bible have influenced our lives today: men like Abraham, Moses, Jacob, Jeremiah, King David, Daniel, Isaiah, the apostles, Paul, and the many leaders of the early church. Each of them made an impact to our lives in the messages and examples of faith they left behind. We read their letters to believers, the recounting of historical events, and prophecies for the future. Through their testimony, we learn about the works and plans of God.

At the beginning of each of the previous chapters, I included a quote from a well-known pastor or spiritual leader. Some of these men have died; others are still living. These men decided to make a difference with their lives and God enabled them to influence generations with their message and ministries.

Each of us will leave an impact, as well. We may never be authors of a book in the Bible, a famous television evangelist, or famous musician, but our voices will affect the lives of our families, friends, co-workers, neighbors, and countless others that God brings into our lives. We have the opportunity to choose whether our lives will be an example of hope and righteousness or whether they will point to a path moving away from God.

Each day that choice is made in the words we speak, the actions we take, the pursuits we choose to occupy our time with, and countless other little decisions we make. These daily decisions add up to a big impact, one that will last much longer than we can even imagine, when we choose to follow God and are obedient to His ways.

In Psalm 112, it says the righteous will be "remembered forever" (verse 6) and their righteousness will "endure forever" (verse 9). Forever is a long time, long after our lives on earth are finished. This far reaching impact is only possible when our hearts are "steadfast, trusting in the Lord" (verse 7). God alone will remove fear, give the righteous victory over their enemy, and give them honor. This can be the final outcome of your life and my life, if we are faithful to trust God.

FAR REACHING IMPACT

None of you know me well, but I'm not a person of wealth or influence. My life is a simple one. I have worked most of my life. I have paid bills, had my struggles and accomplishments, and raised a family with my husband. While I am a hard worker, I don't have any unique skills that others can't replicate. In fact, if there is anything that I've learned with age it is that I can be replaced. So, when I consider having a far-reaching impact on people in my life, this may sound a bit ambitious for such an average individual as myself. You may be thinking it is a bit ambitious for you, as well.

However, a far-reaching impact is exactly the perspective God has in store for His children. While sinful men will be like chaff the wind blows away (Psalm 1:4) and are soon forgotten (Psalm 103:16), God's plan for the righteous is to have a long-lasting impact on future generations. We need to remember that God's view of life is from the perspective of eternity: He sees the past, present, and future. He knows not only the origin of everything, but sees its fulfillment. He knows the beginning and end of our lives, as well, and knows the future beyond our time on this earth.

Consider the words of Psalm 22, "Posterity will serve Him; future generations will be told about the Lord. They will proclaim His righteousness, declaring to a people yet unborn: He has done it!" (verses 30-31). Posterity refers to our offspring continuing to the furthest generations, not just our children and grandchildren, but generations we will never meet, "a people yet unborn." These generations will serve the Lord and be told about Him. The enduring message they will proclaim is a simple one, "He has done it!" What has He done? Jesus, our Savior, has washed away our sins and made it possible for us to have fellowship with God and live with Him forever.

While we don't control how people will respond to the message we share today, we know that every person who receives Christ will receive eternal life. Our job is simply to be faithful stewards of the hope that lies within us and to tell others about the works of God, to teach them to obey God, and to be examples of righteous living. It is God's Spirit who will do the work of transforming hearts, bringing those who hear the message to a saving faith, and guiding and teaching each current and future disciple of Christ.

DAVID'S LEGACY: THRONE ESTABLISHED FOREVER

One of the legacies we see in the Bible is that of King David. David was the youngest son of Jesse, a man in the family lineage of Judah. While several of his older brothers had gone off to war, led by King Saul, David stayed home and tended his father's sheep. While in the fields, David had a lot of time to think about God and to grow in faith. He marveled at God's provision and protection as he encountered bears and lions in the wild.

Meanwhile, Samuel, a prophet of God, received a vision that another man from Jesse's family in Bethlehem would become King of Israel, in place of Saul (1 Samuel 16:1). Obediently, he set out to anoint this new king. When he came to Jesse, his older sons lined up. As Samuel walked by each of them, he said they were not the ones God had chosen. "Are these all the sons you have?" he asked (1 Samuel 16:11). Jesse told him there was one more son tending the sheep in the fields. Jesse called David and upon seeing him, Samuel said, "this is the one" (1 Samuel 16:12) that God has chosen and anointed him. After being anointed as King, David would have to wait several years before ascending to the throne.

When David took supplies to his brothers on the battle field, David heard a Philistine, Goliath, insulting the Israelites and daring any man among them to challenge him. David was surprised by the men's lack of confidence in God to defeat their enemy. Offended by the insults, he was determined to take a stand for God's name. David remembered how God had protected him in the fields and using a sling and stone, killed Goliath (1 Samuel 17:50). After this impressive feat, David began to serve in Saul's army.

God gave David many successes over the enemy and he grew in popularity with the people. This made Saul very jealous and he tried several times to attack David. Eventually he had to leave Saul's presence and go into hiding. During those years, David's trust and dependency on God grew. Eventually Saul was killed in battle and David became king.

David ruled for forty years. He had his faults and shortcomings, but he maintained his faith in God. He wrote many psalms praising and expressing his love and devotion to God. In his psalms, he admitted his vulnerability and dependence on God and showed the way to forgiveness when one had sinned. Through his psalms and life example, he faithfully taught his children and the people of Israel about God.

David had many sons, some who followed God and some who didn't. In a quick look at the 28 generations from King David to the exile to Babylon and then to the birth of Jesus (Matthew 1:6-17), you will see that some of David's future descendants did as God commanded, while others sinned and turned away from God.

During David's reign, the prophet Nathan revealed, "your house and your kingdom will endure forever before Me; your throne will be established forever" (2 Samuel 7:16). After many generations, Jesus was born. He was the one who would fulfill the prophecy and become a king who would rule forever on David's throne. Regardless of the behavior of some of David's children or the descendants who followed, God would be faithful to keep His promise to David.

THE PATH TO LIFE

I don't think I'm overstating its importance in saying that of all the things we leave behind when we die, a legacy of faith will have the most important and long-lasting impact on our families and others we meet.

Since the beginning of creation, God has known the future. Part of His plan was for mankind to share responsibility in teaching future generations about who He is and how we should respond to His holiness. From the early forefathers of faith, God has covenanted with men and women who worship Him in truth, promising blessings for future generations. The plans that God established at the beginning of creation were made with forever in mind, because of this His plans were established in perpetuity.

Each one of us has been impacted by our parents, grandparents, and generations before us. We share physical traits, cultural practices, and values. We take pride in our family tree, cherish memories, and are devoted to a bond of caring and protection for one another. We also recognize that both the good and bad of our past impacts us. If we've been hurt by our family, we know how difficult it is to dig our way out of bad habits, abusive behavior, and a poor self-image. So, it becomes increasingly important that we leave memories and an inheritance of good habits and righteous living for our children and future generations. With God's help and a renewed spirit made possible through the sacrifice of Jesus, we take steps to turn the tide for the future.

How do we do that? First, we teach our children about God, who He is and His attributes and how to worship God. We develop an understanding of what it means for God to be divine and why belief in this superior being is valid and real. We talk about how even though God is far superior to us, that He is alive and actively involved in our lives. We exemplify what it means to have faith and hope in God and how to respond fully to God, with our mind, body, and soul.

Second, we teach how to live holy and righteous lives that are pleasing to God. We build habits of reading God's word, so that future generations can study God's laws and precepts. Through this they can learn how to love God and each other through their thoughts, actions, and words. In every aspect of our existence, we are called to rise above the ways of the world and instead set our eyes on God and His holy standards. In doing this, we please God and incur His blessing.

Our faith lived out by our actions and love for God are the seed to a harvest that will come to fruition in future generations. When we started this series of lessons on the legacy of faith, one of the scriptures we looked at was God's promise to show "love to a thousand generations of those who love [Him] and keep [His] commandments" (Exodus 20:6).

This promise was never dependent on us, but instead it was dependent on God's faithfulness. Obviously, we would not be able to tell a thousand future generations about God, but would be limited by our short life spans on earth. Nor would there be any guarantee that our children, or future generations, would inherit our faith. Our responsibility in this promise was to love God and keep His commandments. It was God, who would keep the promise to show love to future generations. Just as in the lineage of David, God will be faithful to fulfill His promise.

JESUS' LEGACY: SALVATION AND ETERNAL LIFE

A carpenter and simple man lived in the town of Nazareth, named Joseph. Though it had been many generations removed, he was a descendant of King David. His character was described as a "man faithful to the law" and he was engaged to be married to a woman, Mary (Matthew 1:16, 19). Now Joseph and Mary came from many generations of righteous men. In Matthew 1, verses 2 through 17, the lineage of Joseph included Abraham, Isaac, Jacob, and King David among others.

One night an angel came to Mary in a dream. The angel told

her that she would have a baby who would inherit the throne of David and rule forever over his people (Luke 1:26-33). This child would be the Son of God. Even though Mary was not yet married to Joseph and was a virgin, she miraculously became pregnant with a baby boy. Of course, this upset Joseph and he set out to quietly break his engagement to Mary, since he knew he was not the father of the child (Matthew 1:19). An angel came to Joseph and reassured him, confirming that this child was conceived by God. The angel told Joseph to name the child Jesus, since he would save His people (Matthew 1:20-21). Joseph and Mary were soon married and the child was born in Bethlehem, where they had traveled to register in the census ordered by Caesar Augustus (Luke 2:3-4).

Jesus was raised just as any other child. Yet as he grew it became evident that he was a special child. He studied and understood the word of God in a way that was not common. At twelve-years-old he was found in the temple talking with the priests, who were astonished by his understanding (Luke 2:46-47). He continued to grow in favor with God and man (Luke 2:52). When he was in his thirties, his public ministry began. He was baptized by John the Baptist and the Holy Spirit confirmed his calling (Matthew 3:13-17), descending on Him from heaven. A voice from heaven proclaimed "this is My Son, whom I love; with Him I am well pleased." Just as at His birth, once again Jesus' divine nature was revealed.

Jesus was with God at the beginning of creation, He was still God when He was born and lived on this earth, He was God when He was crucified, He was God when He was resurrected, He is God now at the right hand of the Father, and He will be God still when He returns in power and glory and rules for eternity. There was never a time past, present, or future when Jesus was not God. The mystery of Jesus, who is both divine and human, is a foundational truth of the Christian faith. In Galatians 4, we read "But when the set time had fully come, God sent His Son, born of a woman, born under the law, to redeem those under the law, that we might receive adoption to sonship" (verses 4-5). In this verse, we see both the divinity of Jesus and His purpose, redemption.

So why was it necessary for Jesus to live as a man for a short time on this earth? This happened so that Jesus could be an acceptable sacrifice to God, a perfect man without sin, who could pay for our sins. "For this reason, He had to be made like them, fully human in every way, in order that He might become a merciful and faithful high priest in service to God, and that He might make atonement for the sins of the people" (Hebrews 2:17). Jesus lived to pay the price for our sin so that we would never have to be separated from God again. All of this was with a purpose—that those who believed in Him might have eternal life (John 3:16).

ETERNAL LIFE AND FELLOWSHIP

Eternity has always been in the heart of God. When He created man in the garden of Eden, eternal fellowship with mankind was His plan. When Adam sinned, this relationship was broken. No longer would men and women have unbroken fellowship with God, but instead every person on this earth would face eventual death. Jesus changed the doomed course of mankind. With His death and sacrifice to cover our sins, mankind could now inherit eternal life and fellowship with God. God's plan has been restored.

In his letter to Titus, Paul confirmed his, and that which should be every believer's, purpose. The purpose was to "further the faith of God's elect and their knowledge of the truth that leads to godliness—in the hope of eternal life, which God, who does not lie, promised before the beginning of time" (Titus 1:1-2).

Have you ever considered what it will be like to live forever? As a Christian, I have often wondered about what it will be like to have eternal fellowship with Jesus. For some, they may think of heaven as sitting on clouds and playing harps. For others, heaven is an unending worship service where men and women sing praises to God. There are a multitude of scriptures that talk about heaven and give glimpses into eternal life. It is exciting to realize just how alive we will be in heaven as God's eternal purpose is unveiled and how fulfilling our relationship with God will be.

> Since, then, you have been raised with Christ, set your hearts on things above, where Christ is seated at the right hand of God. Set your minds on things above, not on earthly things. (Colossians 3:1-2)

In scripture, we are exhorted to "set our hearts" and "minds on things above" (Colossians 3:1-2). Hope in eternal life is meant to inspire and give us strength (1 Thessalonians 1:3). God has many wonderful things in store for His children. As co-heirs with Christ, we will share the riches of the coming kingdom.

The next time you think about the money and possessions you will leave your children when you die, just remember where the real treasure lies. Everlasting treasure is found in knowing and walking with God. Make sure you are leaving an inheritance they can take with them and have forevermore!

MAKE A DIFFERENCE!

As we read the chapters of this book, many legacies were shared reminding us of individuals in the Bible who chose to follow God. They were individuals just like us. They faced temptations and made mistakes in life, but the overriding and persistent decision was to keep their eyes on God and to walk in faith. Their lives and commitment to God had an impact on their children and future generations. Their impact continues today as we learn from their example.

A. W. Tozer once said, "we do the greatest service to the next generation of Christians by passing on to them undimmed and undiminished that noble concept of God that we received from our Hebrew and Christian fathers of generations past."[9]

Today as we are blessed by the love and unity of faith that we share as a body of believers, let's not keep the message of salvation and this love to ourselves. Let's make a commitment to pick up the gauntlet for future generations. Let's be mindful of the inheritance and legacy we are leaving behind and share the gospel with others. Let's be intentional in setting an example in our lives of making decisions that are sound doctrine, morally pure and good.

Let's make a difference and leave a legacy of righteousness and faith to future generations!

Prayer: Lord, who can fathom the importance of our decisions, how each day matters in Your plan, and both the blessing and opportunity You have placed at our feet. We are so unworthy to respond to the calling to be Your witnesses. It is more than any man or woman can fulfill in their own power. So, Lord, we ask that You keep Your promises and fulfill those things which are impossible for men. We pray, Lord, that we will become Your faithful servants, empowered by Your precious Holy Spirit. We pray You will never leave us but be ever present in our lives. It is in the name of Jesus, who alone is worthy to save, that we pray. Amen.

Reflections and Personal Study

Reflect on the main topics covered in the chapter.
Read and meditate on supporting scriptures.
Consider how this applies to your personal life.

Topic: The importance of the legacy we leave our children is emphasized in its eternal consequence.

Far Reaching Impact

Topic: Posterity will serve him; future generations will be told about the Lord.

Application: Have you ever considered the impact your words and actions have on future generations?

Application: What is the legacy you want to leave behind to your children, your grandchildren, and those in future generations that you will never meet?

David's Legacy

Topic: Through his psalms and life example, he faithfully taught his children and the people of Israel about God.

Scripture: Read 2 Samuel 7:16. What was God's promise to David?

The Path to Life

Topic: With God's help and a renewed spirit made possible through the sacrifice of Jesus, we take steps to turn the tide for the future.

Application: What is a Christian's responsibility toward future generations?

Jesus' Legacy

Topic: He lived to pay the price for our sin so that we would never have to be separated from God again.

Scripture: Read Hebrews 2:17. Why was it important that Jesus be both man and God?

Scripture: Read Galatians 4:4-5 and John 3:16. What was Jesus' legacy to mankind?

Eternal Life and Fellowship

Topic: Everlasting treasure is found in knowing and walking with God.

Application: How does the idea of living forever with Jesus motivate you toward obedience and righteousness?

Make a Difference!

Topic: Let's make a difference and leave a legacy of righteousness and faith to future generations.

Scripture: What can you do today to make a difference for future generations in your family?

ABOUT THE AUTHOR

DeLinda N. Baker was raised as a Christian, but strayed from her faith as a young adult. She attended the University of Texas at Austin and majored in accounting, graduating in 1977 with a bachelor's degree in business.

Toward the end of her sophomore year in college, DeLinda felt the tug of the Holy Spirit and renewed her commitment to follow and live for Jesus. From that day on, her life began to change as God began to work in her life.

Professionally, DeLinda started out in accounting and then became a technical consultant assisting companies in moving manual accounting processes onto computerized systems. For the remainder and bulk of her career, she was a senior project manager for technical, process, and merger initiatives for a major national bank. In this capacity, she moved up in rank until she retired in 2015.

Spiritually however, DeLinda began to discover different gifts and desires. Early in her walk with the Lord, among those gifts, she found she had a deep desire to teach. While initially she led Bible studies developed by other authors, she later began to develop her own studies on topics that plagued Christians and were often misrepresented in our culture. Her passion in teaching is to be true to the Word of God and to not add or subtract from the teachings of scripture.

DeLinda has served as deacon for numerous years in her church, actively participated in the leadership of the women's ministry, led Sunday school classes, and assisted with administrative and financial projects in the church.

ENDNOTES

1   James Strong, *Strong's Exhaustive Concordance of the Bible: With Greek and Hebrew Dictionary* (Nashville, TN, Crusade Bible Publishers, Inc., 1986), "Hebrew and Chaldee Dictionary", pg. 14

2   Merriam-Webster online dictionary, "hope", https://www.merriam-webster.com/dictionary/hope

3   American Bible Society, "Education in Ancient Israel", http://bibleresources.americanbible.org/resource/education-in-ancient-israel

4   American Bible Society, "Education in Ancient Israel", http://bibleresources.americanbible.org/resource/education-in-ancient-israel

5   James Strong, *Strong's Exhaustive Concordance of the Bible: With Greek and Hebrew Dictionary* (Nashville, TN, Crusade Bible Publishers, Inc., 1986), "Greek Dictionary of the New Testament", pg. 75

6   https://www1.cbn.com/cbnnews/us/2019/october/powerful-botham-jeans-brother-forgives-offers-christ-and-embraces-police-officer-who-nbsp-killed-his-brother

7   Merriam-Webster online dictionary, "greed," https://www.merriam-webster.com/dictionary/greed

8   Merriam-Webster online dictionary, "blessed," https://www.merriam-webster.com/dictionary/blessed

9   A. W. Tozer, *The Knowledge of the Holy* (San Francisco, CA, Harper Collins Publishers, 1961)

Printed in the United States
By Bookmasters